A Thirteenth-Century Textbook of Mystical Theology at the University of Paris

The *Mystical Theology* of Dionysius the Areopagite
in Eriugena's Latin Translation with the Scholia translated by
Anastasius the Librarian and Excerpts from Eriugena's *Periphyseon*

DALLAS MEDIEVAL TEXTS AND TRANSLATIONS
4

A Thirteenth-Century Textbook of Mystical Theology at the University of Paris

The *Mystical Theology* of Dionysius the Areopagite in Eriugena's Latin Translation with the Scholia translated by Anastasius the Librarian and Excerpts from Eriugena's *Periphyseon*

EDITION, TRANSLATION, AND INTRODUCTION
BY

L. Michael Harrington
(University of Dallas)

PEETERS
PARIS – LEUVEN – DUDLEY, MA
2004

Cover illustration: illuminated first line of Dionysius' *Mystical Theology*, from MS. *Paris, Bibl. nat., lat. 1618*, fol. 79v. By kind permission of the Bibliothèque nationale de France, Paris.

Library of Congress Cataloging-in-Publication Data

A thirteenth-century of mystical theology at the University of Paris: the Mystical theology of Dionysius the Areopagite in Eriugena's Latin translation, with the scholia translated by Anastasius the Librarian, and excerpts from Eriugena's Periphyseon/edition, translation, and introduction by L. Michael Harrington.
    p. cm. -- (Dallas medieval texts and translations; 4)
Includes bibliographical references (p.).
ISBN 90-429-1394-0 (alk. paper)
    1. Pseudo-Dionysius, the Areopagite. De Mystica theologia. 2. Mysticism--Early works to 1800. I.Anastasius, the Librarian, ca. 810-ca. 878. II. Harrington, L. Michael. III. Pseudo-Dionysius, the Areopagite. De mystica theologia. English & Latin. IV. Eriugena, Johannes Scotus, ca. 810-ca. 877. De divisione naturae. English & Latin. Selection. V. Series.

BR65.D63 D4538 2004
248.2'2--dc22

                                                                    2003063224

© 2004 – Peeters – Bondgenotenlaan 153 – B-3000 Leuven – Belgium.
ISBN 90-429-1394-0
D. 2004/0602/5

For my mother and father

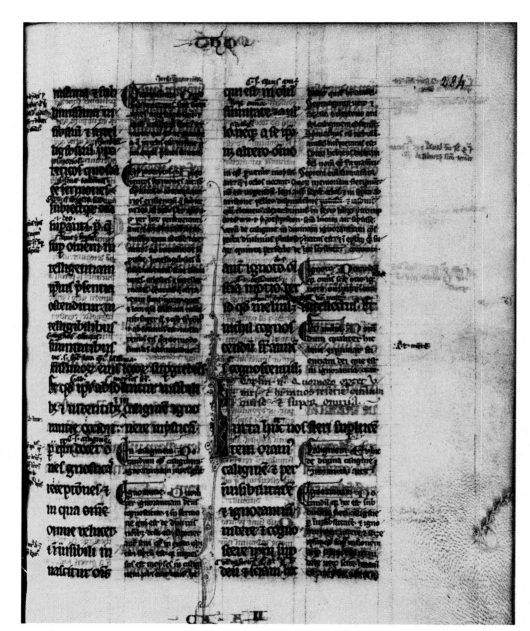

MS. *Paris, Bibl. nat., lat. 17341*, fol. 284r, showing the beginning of the second chapter of the *Mystical Theology.* By kind permission of the Bibliothèque nationale de France, Paris.

Editor's Foreword

The Dallas Medieval Texts and Translations series pursues an ambitious goal: to build a library of medieval Latin texts, with English translations, from the period roughly between 500 and 1500, that will represent the whole breadth and variety of medieval civilization. Thus, the series is open to all subjects and genres, ranging from poetry through philosophy, theology, and rhetoric to treatises on natural science. It will include, as well, medieval Latin versions of Arabic and Hebrew works. In the future, the publication of vernacular texts is a possibility. Placing these texts side by side, rather than dividing them in terms of the boundaries of contemporary academic disciplines, will, we hope, contribute to a better understanding of the complex coherence and interrelatedness of the many facets of medieval written culture.

In consultation with our distinguished board of editorial advisers, we have established principles that will guide the progress of the series. The primary purpose of the Dallas Medieval Texts and Translations is to render medieval Latin texts accessible in authoritative modern English translations; at the same time the series strives to provide reliable texts in Latin where such are not yet available. The translations are therefore established either on the basis of existing good critical editions (which we do not normally reprint) or, when necessary, on the basis of new editions. To enhance the accessibility of the texts to a wide academic public, including graduate students, the critical apparatus of the editions is limited to important variants. Each volume comprises scholarly introductions, notes, and annotated bibliographies.

Works published in the Dallas Medieval Texts and Translations are unexcerpted and unabridged. In the case of a work too long to appear in a single volume, we will start with the beginning of the work or publish integral parts of it, rather than creating a selection of discontinuous texts.

In this fourth volume of our series, readers find an edition and translation that should make an important contribution to a range of debates in contemporary medieval studies. Dr. L. Michael Harrington, of the University of Dallas, has for the first time given us a part of the famous handbook that was used for the study of Dionysian theology at the University of Paris in the thirteenth century — namely, the part devoted to the *Mystical Theology*. Albert the Great is known to have consulted this handbook, and quotations from it also appear in the works of Thomas Aquinas. The significance of this text is comparable to that of the "study guide" from MS. Barcelona, *Ripoll 109*, which has been so vividly discussed in recent years: for it gives us an insight

into the actual techniques of learning — that is to say, of tradition-building — as they were practiced at the early universities. Thus, we see that the *Mystical Theology* and the other Dionysian writings were thoroughly embedded in a context of explanations and commentaries that made them accessible to the contemporary reader in the light of a tradition which had already interpreted them in a certain manner.

Wisely, Dr. Harrington has decided to produce an edition and translation that are as faithful to the manuscripts of the Dionysian textbook as reasonably possible. Thus, his edition attempts to reproduce the layout of one of the principal manuscripts, MS. *Paris, Bibliotheque nationale, lat. 17341*, as well as following the text of this and one other good manuscript witness very closely. In other words, rather than creating an edition of "a text which never existed" — an anomaly that is now recognized as the main danger of classical textual scholarship — Dr. Harrington has opted to show us the medieval text with all its mistakes and oddities: for these have often influenced the reception of the Pseudo-Dionysius significantly.

A central portion of Dr. Harrington's introduction explains the subtle shift that occurred even among Dionysius' earliest commentators; a shift from the clear distinction that Dionysius himself makes between the mystical union and human understanding, toward a redefinition of that union as a transformation or radicalization of intellectual activity. This interpretation as it were takes the edge off Dionysius' radical mysticism, bringing it closer to a philosophy and theology for which God is the summit of all being and intellection

Thanks are due to the University of Dallas, whose financial support has made this series possible. Professor Glen Thurow, formerly Provost and Dean of Constantin College, believed in this project years before the first contributor submitted a manuscript. His successor, Professor Thomas Lindsay, has continued the University's generous assistance. Emmanuel and Paul Peeters enthusiastically embraced the idea for the Dallas Medieval Texts and Translations when we first discussed it with them in 1998. We are very pleased that our series is associated with a publisher and printer of such great tradition and renown. Thanks are also due to the medievalists in the United States and abroad who have agreed to serve on our board of editorial advisers.

Philipp W. Rosemann
August, 2003

Table of Contents

Acknowledgements

The Lynde and Harry Bradley Foundation provided me with financial support while, as a graduate student at Boston College, I began to seek out and purchase manuscripts containing the Anastasian scholia. Dr. Stephen F. Brown, my advisor at Boston College, provided support and guidance as I began to lay the groundwork for critical editions of the scholia. The University of Dallas has generously supported my work on present and future editions with a King's Scholarship for the purchase of manuscripts, and a stipend for the summer of 2002, which allowed me to complete the present work. Dr. Kent Emery, Jr. served as reader for the final draft. Without his comments, the Latin text and my introductory comments to it would be far less precise. I would also like to thank Dr. Philipp Rosemann, the editor of the Dallas Medieval Texts and Translations series, whose suggestions were instrumental in my decision to produce an edition of the *Mystical Theology* in its present format.

Introduction

The *Mystical Theology* came to the court of the Frankish king Louis the Pious in the year 827 as part of a manuscript containing works purported to be written by Dionysius the Areopagite. It was written in Greek, and so was unintelligible to nearly everyone who might want to read it. Copies of the works of Dionysius in Greek had been present in Rome since at least the seventh century, but so far as we know, no one had yet translated them into Latin. This new presentation, a gift from the Byzantine emperor Michael the Stammerer, was special. The Franks believed that Dionysius the Areopagite had founded the abbey of Saint-Denis outside Paris. They were inclined, then, to give an exceptional preeminence to his works. The manuscript was taken to Saint-Denis in a procession on the eighth of October, the eve of the feast day of Dionysius, and deposited at the abbey. Between five and eight years later, Hilduin, the abbot of Saint-Denis, made the first translation of the works of Dionysius into Latin.

Hilduin's translation left much to be desired. G. Théry, who discovered and edited it, believed it to be a collaborative effort on the part of three people.[1] One would decipher the Greek manuscript, which contained no spaces between words and virtually no accent marks. As he deciphered the manuscript, he would read it aloud in Greek. A second collaborator would then orally translate the Greek into Latin, and a third would write down the translation. This collaborative effort, while efficient, may have been the cause of some of the numerous problems with Hilduin's translation. His reading of the Greek was often inaccurate, his translation of Greek terms was highly inconsistent, employing up to sixteen different translations for a single Greek term, and he showed no effort to understand the text he was translating. The translation as a whole proved to be at once too literal, in its word-for-word method, and too vague, in its imprecise and fluctuating choice of translations. It did not circulate widely, and was immediately superseded by Eriugena's version when it appeared thirty years later.

Eriugena was himself already an accomplished theologian when he took up the task of translating Dionysius. His seminal work, *On Divine Predestination*, had gained him notoriety and some dislike within the ecclesiastical community when he composed it around 851 or 852. The Frankish king, Charles the Bald, undeterred by Eriugena's bad press, retained him as his theologian, and invited him to produce a translation of Dionysius which redressed the mistakes of Hilduin. Eriugena's earlier work reflected

---

[1] See G. Théry, *Études dionysiennes*, vol. 1 (Paris: Vrin, 1932), 101–42.

the influence of Origen, and demonstrated his familiarity with Greek thought, but his reading of Dionysius dramatically altered his approach to the Greeks and to theology in nearly all his subsequent work. His translation appeared around 860 to mixed reviews. Like Hilduin's, Eriugena's version was quite literal, but Eriugena employed accurate and consistent translations of Greek terms, and he attempted to understand the mind of Dionysius in a way Hilduin had not. The translation was sent to Rome, where the papal librarian Anastasius expressed both his astonishment that an Irishman could pull off such a feat and his dismay that Eriugena's literal translation had left Dionysius largely unintelligible to a Latin audience. Anastasius found, probably in his own library, a Greek manuscript containing scholia on Dionysius' text. If these scholia had helped Greek readers to understand Dionysius, perhaps a Latin translation of them would help Latin readers to understand Eriugena's translation. Anastasius knew Greek, and was able to translate the scholia into the margins of Eriugena's manuscript himself. Eriugena, meanwhile, went on to produce his own major work, the *Periphyseon*, and at least one commentary on Dionysius, the *Expositions on the Heavenly Hierarchy*. There is no evidence that he ever read the scholia that now filled the margins of his translation.

Eriugena's translation never faded into the shadows as Hilduin's did. Even when John the Sarracen produced in 1167 a colloquial Latin translation that finally made Dionysius intelligible to Latin readers, Eriugena's translation continued to circulate. This was due in part to the very literal character which initially made it a disappointment. Scholars who wanted to get closer to the Greek original could complement their reading of Sarracen with a reading of Eriugena. Eriugena's translation also continued to flourish because of its association with the scholia that now occupied its margins. Anastasius had translated the scholia to match the terms used by Eriugena. It would have been useless to copy them into the margins of someone else's translation, and so they remained the special property of Eriugena's translation. Around the middle of the thirteenth century, an anonymous scholar, possibly a Dominican working in Paris, took this tradition of marginal commentary a step further.[2] He read through Eriugena's own

---

[2] The most famous of the surviving copies of the thirteenth-century edition — MS. *Paris, Bibliothèque nationale, lat. 17341* — belonged to the Dominican convent of Saint-Jacques in Paris. The scribe who copied it wrote *frere dominique* or "Dominican brother" while trying out his pen on folio 241, as noted by H. F. Dondaine, *Le corpus dionysien de l'université de Paris au XIIIᵉ siècle* (Rome: Edizioni di Storia e Letteratura, 1953), 15–6. J. McEvoy, "John Scottus Eriugena and Thomas Gallus, Commentators on the *Mystical Theology*," in *History and Eschatology in John Scottus Eriugena and His Time*, ed. J. McEvoy and M. Dunne (Leuven: University Press, 2002), 183–202, at 201, suggests that MS. 17341 is the progenitor of all the other surviving copies of the thirteenth-century edition. This cannot be the case, however, since many of the other copies are free from its mistakes. See below, p. lx. We cannot then positively conclude that the thirteenth-century edition was produced in Paris by a Dominican simply because MS. 17341 was produced in Paris by a Dominican.

works of philosophy, primarily the *Periphyseon*, and selected from them about one hundred passages of differing length that seemed especially helpful in the interpretation of Dionysius. He added these excerpts to the scholia that already filled the margins of Eriugena's Dionysius translation. Most of the new excerpts went to the *Divine Names* and the *Mystical Theology*. The anonymous editor then changed the format of the manuscript, giving the scholia greater prominence by removing them from the margins and copying them into the same area occupied by Eriugena's translation. Short portions of Eriugena's translation now alternated with passages from his *Periphyseon* and Anastasius' translation of the scholia.

The resulting edition included more than just Eriugena's translation, Anastasius' translation of the scholia, and the *Periphyseon* excerpts. It also contained the later translation of the Dionysian corpus made by John the Sarracen, a paraphrase made by Thomas Gallus, as well as commentaries on the *Heavenly Hierarchy* made by Eriugena, John the Sarracen, and Hugh of St. Victor.[3] In this form Eriugena's translation of Dionysius not only survived, but became a powerful scholarly tool in the later medieval interpretation of Dionysius. It came to be used as a textbook for Dionysian studies at the University of Paris, where it may have originated, and at many other universities and monastery schools.[4] Albert the Great consulted it in Paris while preparing his commentary on the Dionysian corpus. Quotations of the scholia popped up here and there in authors such as Alexander of Hales and Thomas Aquinas. In the fourteenth century, Denys the Carthusian took the remarkable step of basing his own Dionysian commentary on Eriugena's translation rather than the Sarracen's. He explained that Eriugena was a "most learned man, familiar with the Greek idiom," and so had a unique capacity to lead the reader closer to the spirit of Dionysius.[5] The Carthusian's comment became a kind of final tribute to Eriugena's translation, since the coming Renaissance brought with it a number of new, more accurate translations, and Eriugena's translation was finally laid aside. The mystical theology of Dionysius, however, continued to develop and to sustain the interest of the more speculative Renaissance philosophers.[6]

---

[3] See below, p. 34–5.

[4] See Dondaine, *Le corpus dionysien*, 117–22.

[5] See K. Emery, Jr., "A Complete Reception of the Latin *Corpus Dionysiacum*: The Commentaries of Denys the Carthusian," in *Die Dionysius-Rezeption im Mittelalter*, ed. T. Boiadjiev, G. Kapriev, A. Speer (Turnhout: Brepols, 2000), 197–247, at 209.

[6] For a survey of Dionysian influence through the eighteenth century, see art. "Denys l'Aréopagite," in *Dictionnaire de spiritualité* (Paris: Beauchesne, 1935–), vol. 3, 244–429.

MYSTICAL THEOLOGY

As the title of the *Mystical Theology* indicates, the "mystical" is, in at least one of its meanings, a subset of the larger category of theology. The meaning of "mystical" in this sense is then closely tied to the meaning of "theology." Although the English word "theology" remains a virtual transliteration of the Greek θεολογία, the common meaning of the word in English bears little resemblance to the meaning Dionysius gives to the term. Dionysius does not mean by theology a university discipline aimed at preparing future clergy members or educating the laity. He does not even intend the more literal meaning of the term: the study of the nature of God, a common meaning of the term at the time he was writing. Dionysius treats the term not as meaning "words about God," but as meaning "words of God" — that is, the canon of scriptures in the Christian tradition, and, more primarily, the Hebrew tradition. A quick survey of the use of the term "theology" throughout the works of Dionysius reveals that he uses it most often to introduce paraphrases or quotations from the scriptures. For example, he introduces passages from the Christian scriptures with lines such as: "what else is there to learn from holy theology, when it says…."[7] Dionysius is willing to call "theology" his own work and the work of his teachers only insofar as it repeats in a more accessible way the content of the scriptures.[8] So when an anonymous Latin reader of Eriugena's translation wrote above the word "theology": "that is, scripture, when it speaks about God," he gave a definition with which Dionysius would not disagree.[9]

Dionysius is interested in the Hebrew and Christian scriptures primarily as a fabric of names for the divine. As words, all of these names have the same character. They are simply "syllables and pronunciations which do not pass into the thinking soul, but rattle outside on the lips and the hearing."[10] As names, however, they refer to something outside themselves: a meaning. These meanings may be sensuous objects, emotions, or actions, or they may be intelligible structures, or something even higher. As the nature of the meanings differs, so does the nature of the names. Dionysius identifies three different kinds of name, and claims to have written a series of three works which examine them: the *Theological Characters*, the *Divine Names*, and the *Symbolic Theology*. Only the *Divine Names* still exists, and it is likely that the other two works were never written, but form

---

[7] *DN* 122, 2–3 (636C). Page and line numbers refer to the edition of B. R. Suchla, *De Divinis Nominibus* (Berlin: de Gruyter, 1990) and G. Heil and A. M. Ritter, *De Coelestia Hierarchia; De Ecclesiastica Hierarchia; Mystica Theologia; Epistulae* (Berlin: de Gruyter, 1991). All translations are my own.

[8] Dionysius' own work is theology at: *DN* 139, 19 (681A). The writings of his teacher Hierotheus are "second scriptures" at: *DN* 140, 14 (681B).

[9] See below, p. 57.

[10] *DN* 156, 8–10 (708C).

part of Dionysius' fictional chronology of his own life and work. The *Mystical Theology* is the last of Dionysius' theological works, according to his chronology. Hilduin, in his *Passion of St. Dionysius,* calls the *Mystical Theology* a "brief summary of mystical theology," but, in fact, in its third chapter, it is a systematic ordering and summary of every form of theology.[11] Here, Dionysius orders the different forms of theology based on the number of names they contain, and gives a brief description of each one.

The *Theological Characters* describes names which deal with the internal differentiation of the God over being. These are the names of "Trinity," and its differentiation into "Father," "Son," and "Holy Spirit," as well as the names which refer to the Son's entrance into human nature. Aside from the name "Trinity," which is the general name for the internal differentiation, the other names may be defined as names that apply to the over-being without applying to all of it. Of the three sets of names, the *Theological Characters* contains the fewest, because it aims higher than the sensuous world we experience, and higher than the intelligible structure that lies beyond that world. The theological characters aim at the point of least differentiation, the differentiation within the over-being itself.

The title of *On the Divine Names* suggests that the work will cover all the names of God, but it treats only those names which properly refer to the underlying structure of the world that we experience through the senses: names like "being," "life," and "wisdom." Dionysius refers to these here and there as "intelligible divine names" and "bodiless divine names."[12] While we use these names to refer to sensible objects, they do not properly describe the objects themselves, but the structure which underlies them. For instance, we may think of a bird as a being, or a life, but "life" and "being" are not primarily qualities of the bird. They are the structures which underlie both the bird and all else in the world we experience through the senses. Such names hold a twofold difficulty for our understanding. First, they do not properly characterize sensuous objects, and so lie outside our experience, since we can only experience what has a sensuous component. If "being" is removed from the bird that has it, we may still talk about it, but we can no longer experience it. Second, they compress a great deal of content within themselves, since each one of them articulates a structure for the entire world we see. The content of these names, then, is not self-evident to everyone. There are some who have a higher power of understanding, and can contemplate the content of these names directly. Dionysius mentions his teachers, Hierotheus and the apostle Paul, as two such people. It is fitting for such people, he says, to "see the intelligible meanings

---

[11] PL 106: 31C–32A. The thirteenth-century editor excerpted Hilduin's statement as an introduction to Eriugena's translation of the *Mystical Theology*. See below, p. 47.
[12] *DN* 121, 6 (597B); 211, 8 (913B); 231, 7 (984A).

with their own eyes and teach them all in one."[13] The intelligible is like a spinning color wheel, which only someone with a superhuman speed of perception can distinguish into its different colors while it spins. Ordinary humans see only white until they can stop the wheel and distinguish the different colors separately. Dionysius claims for himself only the ability to perform this latter task, of slowing down the spinning color wheel to distinguish its component parts. For him, he says, "the understanding and learning of the meanings that lead to the sight" of the intelligible meanings is the most fitting. In the *Divine Names*, then, he unfolds the content of the intelligible names to overcome our twofold difficulty in understanding them. He uses language more directly associated with sensuous objects, and he breaks down the names into their different aspects, and looks at each aspect on its own. The result is that the reader may ascend from the sensuous, multiple meanings of the names, toward their intelligible, unified meanings. When the names have been purified of their sensuous, multiple meanings, they stand on the threshold of the over-being.

The *Symbolic Theology* describes names which properly refer to sensuous objects, emotions, and actions in our ordinary experience. Dionysius gives us examples like "shape," "place," "grief," "drinking bout," and "sleep." Their meaning remains close to the sensuous, and so they are easily grasped. Since our ordinary experience is directed to action in the sensuous world, and we must grasp the meaning of names and objects in order to act successfully, these names are the most useful for our everyday life. For instance, we must be able fully to grasp the meaning of the names contained in the command, "Beware of dog!" in order to avoid getting bitten. Since these names properly refer to sensuous objects and events, we cannot discover the divine in them by simply unfolding their content. To signify the divine, these names must be placed in a context in which they can be divorced from their proper meaning, and associated with a content external to them. Theology is such a context. When these names appear in theology, it makes no sense to read them as signifying a sensible object or event. The only way to give them sense is to attach them to an external content. One of Dionysius' favorite examples is a verse from the Book of Psalms: "the Lord awoke, like a strong man, powerful but reeling with wine."[14] Here we have two names that describe events familiar to our ordinary experience: "sleep" and "drinking bout." Their very presence within theology suggests the need to look for an external content for them, since the mere understanding of them would not enable us to go beyond ordinary experience. Here, however, the two terms are explicitly applied to the divine, which provides a much more compelling reason to look for an external content, since sensuous names are particularly unsuited to the God above being. Dionysius gives both names an

---

[13] *DN* 140, 17–8 (681C).
[14] Ps. 78:65.

intelligible content. He explains that "sleep" is "God's removal from and lack of communication with the objects of his providence," and "drinking bout" is "the over-loaded measurelessness of all goods in the one who is their cause."[15] Both of these are intelligible contents. They articulate the underlying structure of the sensuous world, without saying anything directly about the sensuous itself. Dionysius invariably relies on such intelligible contents to give the symbolic names a role in theology. In other words, the symbolic names lead the reader to the divine names.

The *Mystical Theology* stands as the fourth and last in this chronology of the theological works. It does not introduce a new set of names, but reverses the sequence followed in the first three works. Rather than descending from the set of the fewest names to the set of the most names, it ascends from the most to the fewest. The *Mystical Theology* also provides a new method of using the names. While the first three treatises apply names to God, the *Mystical Theology* clears these names away. What the first three treatises affirm, the *Mystical Theology* denies. It is not, then, under the burden of unfolding a name into a graspable content, as is the *Divine Names*, or of attaching an extraneous content to a name, as is the *Symbolic Theology*. The *Mystical Theology* is not concerned with content at all, and so its exposition does not require more than the presentation of the names in their new sequence and method.

Dionysius' exposition of mystical theology occupies only the brief fourth and fifth chapters of the work. He begins the ascending series of clearings by denying that God is any of the lower levels of reality. He is not matter ("lacking being"), an element like stone ("lacking life"), or a beast ("unreasoning," "lacking intellect"). The rest of the fourth chapter proceeds to deny that God is or has a body, any of the characteristics of the body, or any of the structural components of the body. Dionysius does not take the trouble of denying the names of the *Symbolic Theology* one by one, saying that God is not "star," not "mixing bowl," and so on. He simply denies that God is the one thing they all have in common: a body. The fifth chapter ascends through the other two forms of name: the divine or intelligible name, and the theological character. Dionysius begins by denying to God the characteristics of the two levels of reality capable of considering these latter two kinds of name: humans ("soul," "imagination," "opinion," "reason") and angels ("intellect," "intelligence"). He then goes on to deny many of the names he discussed in the *Divine Names*. "Size," "smallness," "equality," "likeness," "unlikeness," "stillness," "motion," "power," "light," "life," "substance," "time," "wisdom," "one," "deity," "goodness" — Dionysius unfolds all these names in his *Divine Names* and denies them here in the *Mystical Theology*. Finally, he denies three names from the *Theological Characters*: "spirit," "sonship," and "fatherhood." With the denial of these last three names, Dionysius completes his ascent from the lowest to the highest set of names.

---

[15] *Ep.* IX, 206, 9–10 (1113B); 204, 13–205, 1 (1112C).

Dionysius concludes the *Mystical Theology* with a new claim: that the divinity is over the denials just as much as it is over the affirmations. To say that God is "not being" approaches him no more than to say that he is "being." The *Mystical Theology* does not introduce a new, higher form of name adequate for characterizing the divine. It works within the three existing forms of name, serving to clarify and limit their activity. The *Divine Names* declares that God is being. Without some clarification of how God is being, Dionysius risks becoming one of those "conformed to the things that are," and "imagining that nothing is over realities in a manner over being."[16] The *Mystical Theology* clarifies that God is "being" in such a way that he is also "not being." The closing lines of the *Mystical Theology* realize that, like the other forms of theology, mystical theology may be misunderstood if taken on its own. It needs the other three forms of theology as much as they need it. To say that denials adequately characterize the over-being is to persist in the attempt to characterize the divinity positively, even if the characterization is now "nothing," the negation of our sensuous world and its intelligible foundation. Although Dionysius guards against this possibility in the closing lines of the *Mystical Theology*, he is generally less concerned with it than with the opposite possibility: that God might be conceived as a mere being. The latter concern would have been more relevant to his contemporaries, who were often criticized for having a ridiculously anthropomorphic view of the divine.

The name "mystical," then, can signify the form of theology which denies of God all kinds of predication. This theology remains a form of speaking, since the denials have the form of words, even if they do not make predications of an object. It may also be characterized as instruction, since it reveals a method by which we ought to approach the theological names. There is another side to the name "mystical," derived from the same Greek word μύεω, but closer to its essence than the more general meaning of "to instruct." The kind of instruction presented in the ancient mystery cults, where the term "mystical" first arose, was an initiation, and was not to be communicated to the uninitiated.[17] Because of this association with secret knowledge, the term "mystical" acquired the additional signification of "secret." For Dionysius, of course, this meaning of "mystical" does not simply characterize his mystical theology, but all theology. In the *Divine Names* he warns Timothy "not to make the divine things known to the uninitiated."[18] The *Heavenly Hierarchy* and the *Ecclesiastical Hierarchy* also contain such admonitions.[19] Dionysius, then, does not give "mystical" the meaning of "secret," since

---

[16] *MT* 142, 13–4 (1000A).
[17] For a discussion and brief bibliography on the Greek mysteries, see W. Burkert, *Greek Religion* (Cambridge, Mass.: Harvard University Press, 1985), 276–290.
[18] *DN* 121, 15 (597C).
[19] *CH* 145C; *EH* 377A–B.

all his theology is secret. He does, however, retain the sense of "unspoken" that characterizes this use of "mystical." The theme of silence runs through the *Mystical Theology*, especially in the first and third chapters.

We have seen how the higher sets of names, like the theological characters, contain fewer names than the lower sets, such as the symbolic names. The Christian who uses the practice of mystical theology to ascend through these sets of names will find himself with fewer and fewer names as they approach what they describe. So far we have considered mystical theology only as a method of using the names contained in the three other forms of theology, a method which gives them a dynamism that frees them from the illusion of grasping their object. Dionysius, however, also tells us that the ascent through the names terminates in something other than naming. At the conclusion of the ascent, abandoning the names found in the *Theological Characters*, "as we enter into the very darkness above thought, we find not little speech, but a failure of speech and naming." He continues, a little later, with a description of what happens to our speech after it passes through the pathless regions of the theological characters: "after all the pathless, it will be wholly without a voice, and wholly united to the one who lacks sound." The ascent through clearing away the names of God terminates in what is not an act of speech at all. Dionysius characterizes it rather as an absence of speech, "a failure of speech and naming." He characterizes the act of the Christian who reaches this stage as an "entrance," a word which has no cognitive implication, and so is appropriate for what is not an act of knowing.

This description of the final stage of theology as lying outside of naming and knowing is not a unique aberration on Dionysius' part. In the first chapter of the *Mystical Theology*, he has already described at greater length the ascent through naming and out of naming into the darkness of silence and unknowing. In this earlier description, he uses a scriptural figure to illustrate the ascent: the ascent of Moses up Mount Sinai. In this description, Dionysius calls the highest stage of the ascent, the stage of silence and unknowing, the "truly mystical."

The ascent begins with a preliminary purification. We may be reminded of the purification of baptism which separates those within the church from those outside, or the purification which frees the soul from attachments to material things, but Dionysius may also be taking his cue from Exodus, where God commands the Israelites to be sanctified and to clean their clothes before Moses ascends the mountain.[20] After this purification, Moses has an experience characterized first and foremost as an experience of the senses: he hears trumpets, and he sees lights. It is also characterized by its multiplicity: the trumpets are of "many voices," there are many lights, and the rays are of "many outpourings." There is nothing impure about these visions, though they are

---

[20] See Ex. 19:10.

sensuous and multiple, since Moses has already been purified. They are, however, only the beginning of the ascent. Most of the people remain here, but Moses goes beyond them, ascending to the summit with his chosen priests. Here on the summit Dionysius pauses for another description. Dionysius identifies this summit as "intelligible," in contrast to the sensuous nature of the earlier visions. The very idea of a summit also connotes a unity in contrast to the multiplicity of the earlier sensuous visions. We have here, then, the unitary and intelligible rather then the multiple and sensuous. This, Dionysius says, is not God, but "the place where he has stood."[21] God cannot be contemplated, but this is the place of contemplation. It is the place where the presence of God is shown, "a presence which paces over the intelligible summits of his most holy places." The presence of God, then, is not the same as God himself. We may be aware of his presence, study it, and know it, but God himself escapes this cognitive act. When Moses and his priests contemplate the presence of God on the summit of Mount Sinai, they know God in the only way possible, but their knowledge is oblique.

Dionysius has borrowed the term "summit" from the Hebrew scriptures, where it literally describes the top of Mount Sinai where Moses stands. It is, then, a symbolic name, and Dionysius follows his usual practice of giving the symbolic name an intelligible content. He says that "summit" indicates "certain underlying meanings." These meanings are "the most divine and loftiest of things seen, thought, and subject to the one who transcends all." Every meaning indicated by a name is a link in a hierarchically ordered chain of all the meanings indicated by the name. For instance, when I apply the name "being" to a bird, I refer to a thing which is higher than a stone, but lower than many other objects to which I could apply the same name, such as humans and angels. The highest object to which I can apply the name is the "underlying meaning" of the name. The underlying meaning of "being" is the loftiest of all beings, both those that can be seen and those that can only be thought of. It, like them, is subject to "the one who transcends all." These highest meanings, the underlying meanings which form the exemplary instances of the world we experience, take us to the threshold of the over-being itself. It is tempting to identify them as components of the over-being. This, however, renders meaningless the separation of the summit, the place of God, from the darkness above it, which is God himself. If the underlying meanings were the over-being, then the over-being would itself enter the realm of meaning, and so could in principle be grasped, breaking down the distinction between understanding and the union that surpasses it.

To stand on the summit, in this intelligible place, is the prerogative of those who can "see the intelligible meanings with their own eyes," like Hierotheus, or the chosen priests of Moses. Dionysius and Timothy remain down below, among the lights and sounds, the "meanings that lead to the sight" of this intelligible place. Although this summit is the top

---

[21] Ex. 24:10.

of the mountain, Dionysius posits a further stage. Access to this stage is gained not by a further ascent, but by being "freed from" the sensuous and intelligible, and "entering" the truly mystical. Here is the problem for our earlier interpretation of mystical theology, which integrates it into the practice of the other forms of theology. In his account of Moses, Dionysius separates the mystical, as though temporally, from the sensuous and intelligible activities which ground the other forms of theology. "And then," he says, after contemplating the place where God has stood, Moses enters the mystical darkness. In the darkness, Moses abandons the basis not only of the other forms of theology, but of all theology: speech and naming. He abandons the awareness that is the mind's successful interaction with meaning. The mind itself, in fact, ceases to be active, so that it can be united with what cannot be known. Moses then "is of what is beyond all things, and is of nothing, neither himself nor another." Dionysius characterizes this stage as absolute negation, a rejection of both sensation and thought, the components of human experience.

In both the first and third chapters of the *Mystical Theology*, Dionysius characterizes this stage with the term εἰσδύω, or "enter into." We "enter the darkness over intellect"; Moses "enters the truly mystical darkness." The term has no use in descriptions of cognitive activity, and Dionysius may have chosen it for just this reason. The term literally describes a sensuous action. Its root, δύω, can describe the putting on of clothes, the entrance into a place, or the rushing into battle. These activities do not require conscious attention to them. A sleepwalker may enter a place without being conscious of it at all. We may only acquire the courage to rush into battle by actually putting the thought of it out of our minds, and rushing blindly in. The term "to enter into," or εἰσδύω, in the *Mystical Theology* has an exact parallel in the term "rush toward," or ἐπιβάλλω, in the *Divine Names*, where Dionysius also discusses the three-tiered ascent from sense, to intellect, to what is beyond intellect. This latter term Dionysius borrows directly from a passage in the writings of the third-century Neoplatonist Plotinus. A close comparison of Dionysius and Plotinus in their use of this non-cognitive language helps to answer one of the major questions in recent scholarship on the *Mystical Theology*: is mystical union in the soul's power? In other words, does the soul have a faculty for union with God? The assumption behind the question is that, if the soul has a faculty for union, then the union is active and manipulable on the part of the human soul.[22] The resolution of this question requires an understanding of the "entrance" or "onrush" and the extent to which it is an activity of the soul.

---

[22] The question is first posed in J. Vanneste, *Le mystère de Dieu* (Brussels: Desclée de Brouwer, 1959), 206. Vanneste, 209, answers in the affirmative. His conclusion has been criticized by J. Rist, "Mysticism and Transcendence in Later Neoplatonism," *Hermes* 92 (1964): 213–25, at 219; and A. Golitzin, *Et Introibo ad Altare Dei* (Thessalonica: Patriarchikon Idruma Paterikon Meleton; George Dedousis, 1994), 109–12.

The Plotinian Background of Dionysius' Mystical Union

Whether Dionysius had access to whole treatises by Plotinus, or only to long excerpts, he was clearly familiar with *Ennead* VI.7.35, where Plotinus uses the term "onrush" (ἐπιβολή) to describe the mind's union with its prior. Unmistakable paraphrases of it appear in at least two sections of the *Divine Names*. We find the longer of the two paraphrases near the beginning of the seventh chapter, where Dionysius cautions the reader not to take what is beyond us as though it were "of our kind." To do so is to deceive ourselves. He then tells us to distinguish our power of understanding from our power of union: "we must understand that our mind has a power to understand, through which it sees the intelligibles. It also has a union which transcends the nature of the mind, through which it is joined to what is beyond it."[23] This statement is a paraphrase of Plotinus, *Ennead* VI.7.35: "the mind, then, has a power to understand, through which it looks at what is inside it. It also has a power by which it looks at what is beyond it, by a kind of onrush and reception." Dionysius has made slight, perhaps unconscious, modifications to the Plotinian passage. He radicalizes the difference between the two roles of mind, by avoiding the terms "power" and "sight" when describing the higher role of the mind. He also changes the object of the mind's understanding from "what is inside it" to "the intelligibles," which may not be inside the mind at all. This latter modifaction is necessary to account for the changed context in which Dionysius refers to the two roles of the mind. He is speaking specifically of our human mind. Plotinus is speaking of the universal mind, whose thought precedes any particular human thought.

Plotinus gives his universal mind two roles because he intends to explain not only how it thinks, but also how it comes into existence. For its thinking, the universal mind does not need objects outside itself. When it thinks, it thinks itself: it "looks at what is inside it." Before it can look at what is inside it, it must first exist. The universal mind does not cause itself to exist, since it is a duality between thinker and object of thought which constitutes the universal mind. That is, it looks at unity while it is itself a unity, and by looking, it comes to be the duality of mind. Plotinus describes this form of looking with the two terms "onrush" (ἐπιβολή) and "reception" (παραδοχή). The term "onrush" depicts the nascent mind as active in its own creation, rushing at the unity which is its source. The other term, "reception," describes the nascent mind as passive, receiving its own existence from its source. Plotinus does not choose between the two terms. The mind depends on unity in order to exist, but it is not merely the passive recipient of existence. It must actively seek its own existence through the onrush.

---

[23] *DN* 194, 10–2 (865C–D).

Dionysius adopts these two terms, "onrush" and "reception," in a passage from the first chapter of the *Divine Names*, where he claims that the one beyond being cannot be thought.[24] He seems to expect the reader to respond with the objection that the angels must surely be able to think the one beyond being, since their powers of thought are much greater than ours. Dionysius answers this objection: "even the unions of the holy powers — should we call them 'onrushes' or 'receptions' of that goodness beyond unknowing and appearance? — are ineffable and unknowable." The Dionysian angels are, with some qualification, analogous to the particular minds that make up the Plotinian universal mind. Their interaction with their source, the "goodness beyond unknowing," is not an act of thought. It is rather a union, which we can call either "onrush" or "reception." Although Dionysius has adopted these terms from Plotinus, he modifies the Plotinian context slightly in the lines that follow: "they exist only in those angels who are made worthy of them by going beyond angelic knowledge." The Plotinian mind, simply by virtue of being a mind, has already united with the one beyond being. If it had not done so, it would not exist as a mind. Existence and unity are more detached from each other in the Dionysian angel. Every angel exists, but not every angel is united to the one beyond being.

One possible reason for this detachment is that the Dionysian angel is closer to the soul than the Plotinian mind is. The soul, for both Dionysius and Plotinus, differs from the mind by the detachment of its activities from one another in its present state. The soul has the ability to be united with the one beyond being, but it does not undertake this unity at the same time as it thinks the intelligibles with its mind, or senses the world around it. It moves from one activity to another. The soul, then, like the angel, has its existence detached from its unity. A few lines up from his description of the angelic unities, Dionysius holds out the hope that one day, when we have become "undecaying and immortal," we will possess all our activities at once. Our eyes will see the visible, our mind will participate in the intelligible, and we will also participate "a union beyond mind in the unknowable and blessed onrushes of the rays beyond appearance."[25] The onrush, then, is not for the angels alone. Our own minds have the capacity for it, too, as we have already seen Dionysius indicate in the seventh chapter. This simultaneity of activity, however, in which the onrush occurs at once with thought and sensation, is only a hope for the future. For the present, Dionysius says, we can only move from one activity to another. First we sense, then we think, and finally we "make an onrush into the ray beyond being, so far as we may." The Dionysian soul presently exists without the constant activity of the onrush. The onrush, then, must not be the necessary condition for its existence, but its

---

[24] See *DN* 116, 9-13 (593B).
[25] *DN* 115, 1–3 (592C).

indescribable completion. So, too, for the Dionysian angel. The onrush which unites it to the one beyond being is an addition to its existence, rather than a condition for its existence. This departure from Plotinus may be a result of Christian influence. Perhaps the idea of the angels participating as active partners in their own creation seemed to liken them too much to the many gods of the Hellenic tradition. Dionysius may also have simply developed the framework of later Neoplatonists like Iamblichus and Proclus on this point. For Iamblichus and Proclus, beings higher than human souls also include in themselves some form of space and time, both of which may serve as a force to differentiate existence from activity.[26] The angels may experience a form of time which distinguishes the moment in which they exist from the moment in which they undertake the onrush.

   Plotinus, on the other hand, is clear that the onrush of the universal mind is not distinct from its own existence as a mind. He asks rhetorically: "does that mind see in part, seeing some things at one time and others at another? Or not? It is rather that our reasoning, in order to teach, makes it come about this way, but the mind always has its thinking and it always has its not thinking, but seeing in that other way." We can understand the mind only by distinguishing its two roles as though they could be performed separately, but this separation is a consequence of the way our understanding works, and not the way that the universal mind works. Plotinus does not extend this simultaneity of activity to the soul. The soul, unlike the mind, interacts with unity in a temporally conditioned way. The soul has its own kind of thought, distinct from the thought of the universal mind. Soul thinks by "confusing and obscuring the mind in it which remains unconfused." Plotinus immediately clarifies what he means by this, and begins to articulate the soul's ascent from its own form of knowing: "the mind of the soul sees first, but the vision comes also to the soul and the two become one." There are two forms of seeing, that of the mind and that of the soul. The two are not essentially different, and may become one. When the soul has become identified with its mind, then the two are ready for an interaction with the good itself, which "raises them so much that they are not in place." Plotinus describes this union with the good in temporal terms, saying that "then" the soul "is not moved, because the good is not moved. It is not soul, because the good does not live, but is above life. It is not mind, because the good does not think. For it ought to become like the good, and if the good does not think, then neither does the soul." In this compact description of the soul's ascent to the good, Plotinus also intimates the original descent which allowed this later ascent. The mind had to see first, and it did this by an onrush into the good. Soul, later, came to see by obscuring the vision of the mind. The existence of the soul, then, depends on the prior existence of the mind, which itself only comes to exist by its

---

[26] See P. C. Plass, "Timeless Time in Neoplatonism," *Modern Schoolman 55* (November, 1977): 1–19.

onrush, an onrush which is continually occurring. The soul itself undertakes this onrush only by restoring itself to identity with its mind. It then goes beyond mind to identify itself with the good outside of sense and thought.

Can we say, then, that union with the over-being is in the soul's power? Do we have a faculty for such union? If we mean by "faculty" a capacity of the soul, like sensation or thought, which can be put into action without the intimate involvement of a higher power, clearly no such faculty for union can be found either in the works of Dionysius or in *Ennead* VI.7.35 of Plotinus. If, on the other hand, we mean by "faculty" the soul's own ability to unite with something higher in such a way that it becomes something prior to soul, then we do find such a faculty in both Dionysius and the passage from Plotinus. Such a faculty, however, strains the meaning of the term as we typically understand it. Ordinarily, the use of a faculty does not change the nature of the being which puts it into action.

The interpreters of Dionysius did not preserve his Plotinian conception of the soul's union with its prior. The tension involved in articulating a possibility for the soul which is not an experience of the soul, undertaken by the mind yet not a mental act, and caused by the soul only when it ceases to be a soul, proved to be more than they wished to maintain. They generally resolved the tension either by reducing the union to an act of intellect, or by enriching it with the language of experience.[27] These resolutions can be found in both Greek and Latin interpreters of Dionysius. The second, "experiential" resolution emerged later than the first, and falls outside the compass of this volume. In the West, it began with Thomas Gallus and the Victorine school in the early thirteenth century, and continued into the Renaissance with Marsilio Ficino. In the East, it centered around Gregory Palamas and the Hesychast movement in the fourteenth century. Both the Latin and Greek interpreters in this tradition, inspired by commentaries on the Song of Solomon, explained Dionysian union as an experience analogous to sensation, though occurring through spiritual and not bodily senses.[28]

The first, "intellectual" resolution appeared earlier in the history of Dionysian interpretation and, in one way or another, can be found in each of the contributors to the thirteenth-century edition of Eriugena's Dionysius translation. The intellectuals observed that the mind is the place where union occurs, and understandably concluded that the union is an activity of the mind. After all, in the first chapter of the *Mystical*

---

[27] B. McGinn calls these the "speculative" and "affective" traditions respectively. See *The Flowering of Mysticism* (New York: Crossroad, 1998), 76.

[28] On the initial formulation of spiritual senses in the work of Origen, see K. Rahner, "The 'Spiritual Senses' according to Origen," in his *Theological Investigations*, vol. 16 (New York: Seabury, 1979), 92–100; B. McGinn, *The Foundations of Mysticism* (New York: Crossroad, 1991), 121–4. On its development in medieval mysticism and its controversial nature therein, see McGinn, "The Language of Inner Experience in Christian Mysticism," *Spiritus* 1 (Fall, 2001): 156–71.

Theology, Dionysius himself says that Moses, in the state of union, "knows over all things," and that the darkness over being "teaches" us. Other statements of Dionysius that posit a radical distinction between thought and union must be filed down significantly for this interpretation to hold. This method of filing down the distinction between thought and union so as to reveal their identity found its most developed expression in the commentaries of Albert the Great and his student, Thomas Aquinas. In the West, however, it began much earlier, with Eriugena's translation of Dionysius into Latin. As we will see, Eriugena's very translation of the *Mystical Theology* eliminates important distinctions between thought and union in Dionysius' text. In the East, the first method of interpretation began even earlier, in the first commentators on Dionysius, and so it is to them that we now turn.

THE GREEK SCHOLIA

The first major commentary on the work of Dionysius began as a set of scholia, probably written into the margins of a manuscript containing Dionysius' works. In the most complete edition, the one printed in the fourth volume of J. P. Migne's *Patrologia Graeca*, the scholia are clearly the work of many authors. Their identity is only slightly less mysterious than the identity of Dionysius himself. Most recent scholarship on the Dionysian scholia has focused on two tasks: (1) identifying the first major contributor to the scholia; (2) identifying the scholia that belong to him. The first of these tasks is less difficult. Although later sources attribute the scholia entirely to Maximus the Confessor, or to both Maximus and John of Scythopolis, the earliest sources attribute them solely to John. These sources are four Greek manuscripts containing an early reading of the scholia.[29] Their attribution is corroborated by a Syriac translation of the scholia made in the eighth century.[30] There seems to be no reason to doubt the attribution of the earliest scholia to John.

A number of scholars also believe they have accomplished the second task: to find out which scholia John wrote.[31] The four Greek manuscripts and the Syriac translation which identify John as their author also contain a roughly equivalent number of

---

[29] Discovered by B. R. Suchla: "Die sogenannten Maximus-Scholien des Corpus Dionysiacum Areopagiticum," in *Nachrichten der Akademie der Wissenschaften in Göttingen, Philologisch-historische Klasse* (1980), 3: 33-66.

[30] Discovered by H. U. von Balthasar: "Das Scholienwerk des Johannes von Scythopolis," *Scholastik* 15 (1940): 16–38.

[31] See von Balthasar, "Das Scholienwerk"; Suchla, "Die sogenannten Maximus-Scholien,"; P. Rorem and J. Lamoreaux, *John of Scythopolis and the Dionysian Corpus: Annotating the Areopagite* (Oxford: Clarendon Press, 1998).

scholia: about six hundred in all. Migne's edition, on the other hand, drawn from later manuscripts, contains about one thousand six hundred scholia. On the basis of this evidence, it seems reasonable to conclude that the six hundred scholia of the earliest manuscripts belong to John of Scythopolis, while the additional thousand scholia in Migne are additions made by later authors. This conclusion assumes that the six hundred scholia of the earliest manuscripts are the work of the first author to comment on the Dionysian corpus. If this is correct, then all subsequent manuscripts should contain these six hundred scholia. They may contain additional scholia added by later authors, but these six hundred should also be present. If a manuscript were discovered which contained only some of the six hundred scholia, it would frustrate this conclusion, raising the alternative possibility that the six hundred scholia are not the work of a single author, but already a compilation made from the work of several authors. An author, or group of authors, produced a set of scholia, numbering perhaps around four hundred, which was copied here and there so as to survive for a few centuries at least. Later, this set of scholia was supplemented with the scholia of another author or group of authors to produce a set of around six hundred scholia. This set of scholia was widely disseminated, so that it became the dominant tradition — the one we find in the four Greek manuscripts and the Syriac translation. The other, minority tradition, of four hundred scholia, gradually disappeared from the scene.

To demonstrate that this alternative conclusion is possible, we need to find at least one representative of the minority tradition. Anastasius the Librarian's Latin translation of the scholia seems to have been made from such a representative. The Anastasian scholia contain only four hundred and twenty complete translations of the six hundred scholia found in the four Greek manuscripts and Syriac translation.[32] There are two possible reasons for this discrepancy: (1) Anastasius was working from a manuscript in the minority tradition; (2) Anastasius was working from a manuscript with the full six hundred scholia in it, but he himself or an earlier Greek scribe omitted around one hundred and eighty whole scholia or portions of them for content or space related reasons. If the latter alternative is correct, then no minority tradition need exist, and we may confidently attribute all six hundred scholia found in the four Greek manuscripts and Syriac translation to John of Scythopolis. Anastasius, however, does not seem to have omitted significant numbers of scholia for reasons of either content or space. If Anastasius had found objectionable scholia among the six hundred and omitted them, we should find a pattern in the content of the "omitted" scholia. They should contain doctrines objectionable or at least unfamiliar to Latin readers. We do not find such doctrines in more than two or three of the one hundred and eighty "omitted" scholia,

---

[32] The Anastasian scholia lack 32 whole scholia from the 600 in the early tradition, and lack significant portions of over 150 others. I count as significant any absence of more than a line of Migne's text.

and so cannot conclude that Anastasius edited them for content.[33] If he had edited the scholia for space related reasons, we should find more "omissions" where the scholia are longer and denser. In fact, the "omissions" occur just as frequently where the scholia are brief and sparse. Anastasius does, then, appear to have worked from a representative of the minority tradition.

We may conclude from this examination of the Anastasian scholia that John of Scythopolis was not the author of all six hundred scholia found in the Greek manuscripts and Syriac translation, since the six hundred scholia are already a compilation of several authors' work. John was the author of some or all of a first set of scholia on the Dionysian corpus. This set of scholia became the minority tradition, which survived long enough that Anastasius could find a copy of it, probably in the papal library, in the ninth century. John of Scythopolis, then, is the author of at least some scholia in the minority tradition, but we cannot confidently attribute any given scholium to him. Even less are we able to find authors for the rest of the scholia: any remaining scholia in the minority tradition, the additional scholia in the Greek manuscripts and Syriac translation, the accumulation of later scholia found in Anastasius' translation, and the continuing accumulation gathered by Balthasar Corderius in the edition printed in Migne's *Patrologia Graeca*. In what follows I will not guess at the authorship of particular scholia, but will refer simply to "the scholiasts."

Their different origins do not prevent many of the scholia from manifesting a certain community of thought, which allows us to investigate them as a group. The scholiasts are generally philologists and dogmatists, seeking to employ Dionysius as an authoritative text in resolving the sixth-century controversies over the nature of Christ. The scholiasts show an interest in philology in the *Mystical Theology* to the point that their scholia sometimes depart entirely from their context. One examines the darkness that Moses entered, and goes into the Hebrew word as found in Exodus, its Greek translations, and several interpretation of it as describing the seven firmaments of the heavens.[34] Another scholium, on Dionysius' "conditional affirmation," provides a list of various kinds of conditional and affirmative arguments, drawn from the science of rhetoric.[35] When commenting on Dionysius' claim that the "cause of all things says a lot," the scholiast explains how the Greek word for "says a lot" can carry different meanings depending on where the accent is placed, and he cites a line from Homer to back up his claim.[36] Perhaps it is the same scholiast who later finds parallels in

---

[33] See M. Harrington, "Anastasius the Librarian's Reading of the Greek Scholia on the Pseudo-Dionysian Corpus," in *Studia Patristica*, vol. 36 (Leuven: Peeters, 2001), 119–25.
[34] *PG* 4: 421.1 (p. 69, below).
[35] *PG* 4: 425.11 (p. 89, below).
[36] *PG* 4: 420.3 (p. 65, below).

Euripides, Homer, and Dionysius the Poet for Dionysius' phrase: "statue that is so by nature."[37]

The dogmatic interests of the scholiasts include the demonstration of Dionysius' authenticity, his compatibility with the Hebrew and Christian scriptures, and his orthodox position in the doctrinal controversies of the sixth century. The fact that Dionysius mentions the apostle Bartholomew in the *Mystical Theology* is enough to convince the scholiast that "these divine works of Dionysius are no fiction."[38] The scholiasts rely on the same kind of evidence throughout the works of Dionysius to conclude that he must be who he says he is. They also attempt to situate Dionysius more securely within the embrace of the Hebrew and Christian scriptures. In the *Mystical Theology*, Dionysius quotes the scriptures explicitly only once. The scholia provide references and quotations for Dionysius' implicit use of the scriptures, and attempt to show how his claims are compatible with certain passages of scripture.[39] The purpose of defending Dionysius' identity and compatibility with scripture is so that he may then be used as an authority in the doctrinal conflicts of the sixth century. The scholia attempt to situate Dionysius within these conflicts usually by annotating certain passages with the claim: "note that this opposes the Nestorians and Acephali." The Nestorians and the Acephali both held unorthodox positions on the nature of Christ, the Nestorians dividing his person, and the Acephali uniting his natures. The councils of the church opted for a position between the two, and the scholiast attempts to find in Dionysius evidence for this position. In the *Mystical Theology*, we find such scholia only once.[40]

Their historical and dogmatic orientation does not prevent the scholia entirely from engaging in philosophical development. Some of the scholia betray a background in Neoplatonism. Like Dionysius, at least one of the scholiasts had in front of him either a complete copy of Plotinus' *Enneads* or a set of substantial excerpts from them. The scholia on the *Divine Names* quote passages from Plotinus at length and with little modification.[41] The scholia on the *Mystical Theology* do not quote Plotinus, but do refer to Platonism. One scholium comments on Dionysius' claim that Timothy should abandon "the sensuous, the unseen, every non-being and every being." The scholiast

---

[37] *PG* 4: 421.4 (p. 75, below).
[38] *PG* 4: 420.2 (p. 65, below). Anastasius garbles this passage in his Latin translation of it.
[39] *PG* 4: 416.7 (p. 57, below); 424.3 (p. 85, below); 428.1 (p. 91, below); 429.3 (p. 107, below).
[40] *PG* 4: 425.2. See Appendix A. For a discussion of the scholiasts' pairing of the Nestorians and the Acephali, see Rorem and Lamoreaux, *John of Scythopolis*, 74–7; P. Rorem, "The Doctrinal Concerns of the First Dionysian Scholiast, John of Scythopolis," in *Denys l'aréopagite et sa postérité en Orient et en Occident*, ed. Y. de Andia (Paris: Institut d'Études Augustiniennes, 1997), 187–200, at 193.
[41] For a list of such passages, see R. Frank, "The Use of the *Enneads* by John of Scythopolis," *Le Muséon* 100 (1987): 101–8.

claims that the pairing of sensuous and unseen means the same thing as the pairing of non-being and being, since "the ancients especially called the sensuous itself 'unreality,' since it participates in all kinds of change and does not always remain alike. Now they called intelligibles 'realities,' as I have often said, since, by their maker's will, they are immortal and do not always change their being."[42] The "ancients" here are the Platonists.

Alhough the scholiasts do not refer to the Neoplatonists explicitly when commenting on the *Mystical Theology*, a significant shift in Neoplatonism makes itself felt in their scholia. As we have seen, Plotinus claims that the mind's onrush at the One must transcend its power of thought. Certain other Platonists, such as Plotinus' student Porphyry, do not seem to have preserved this distinction, restoring the identity of unity and thought.[43] Whether or not any of the scholiasts read Porphyry, a crude version of his identification of the One and the universal mind appears in their work. One of the scholiasts, commenting on the *Divine Names*, provides a lengthy quotation from Plotinus' *Ennead* V.9, which describes the character of the universal mind.[44] The scholiast changes the context of the quotation so that it describes God. The characteristics which Plotinus applies to the universal mind in this passage, such as pure act, are now characteristics of God. With this change of context, the distinctive character of Plotinian Neoplatonism is overturned, as the One over being is conflated with the universal mind.

This change of context is reflected in the scholiasts' treatment of the soul's ascent through the forms of knowing into the silence beyond knowing. For Plotinus and Dionysius, the final stage of this ascent is an "onrush," the mind's reaching beyond itself, which takes the form of a self-silencing. The scholiasts preserve the silence of this ascent, but they eliminate its ecstatic element. The mind no longer reaches beyond itself, and it remains mind. The scholiasts resolve the tension in Dionysius' description of union with the over-being by assimilating it to thought. Unknowing becomes a form of knowing.

We find an important first statement of the nature of unknowing early in the scholia on the *Divine Names*.[45] Dionysius has named God "unknowable." The scholiast takes this opportunity to explain that God "becomes known to unknowing." The scholiast distinguishes three meanings of unknowing, only one of which is suitable to the kind of unknowing that knows God. The first kind of unknowing is ignorance, which is "a darkness of the soul," since it is constituted by absence of knowledge. We are in this state of unknowing with respect to all objects we have not heard of, and with respect to those we

---

[42] *PG* 4: 417.2 (p. 59, below).
[43] See P. Hadot, "La métaphysique de Porphyre," in *Porphyre*, ed. H. Dörrie, J.-H. Waszink, W. Theiler (Geneva: Vandœuvres, 1966), 127–63.
[44] *PG* 4: 320.3.
[45] *PG* 4: 216.10. See Appendix B.

have heard of but know nothing about. The second kind of unknowing is "a form of knowledge," the kind of knowledge "that understands that the unknowable is unknown." We are in this state of unknowing when, using our ordinary discursive faculties of knowing, we realize that we cannot know certain things, like the infinite, for example. The third kind of unknowing is what the scholiast is seeking: "the kind of unknowing by which the unknowable is known." The scholiast defines this kind of unknowing by contrasting it with our ordinary faculty of knowing. We exercise our ordinary faculty by a process of scattering and gathering. I come to know what a triangle is by scattering it into its parts, and then gathering those parts back together into a comprehension of the whole. I come to have a certain knowledge of God by scattering him into his parts — like "being," "life," and "intellect" — and then gathering those parts back into a unitary comprehension of God. The trouble with this unitary comprehension is that it is still composed of parts, even if they have been gathered into one. Unknowing seeks a higher form of unity: the perfectly simple. We achieve this simplicity "when we overcome all thought of God." Such simplicity allows us to "remain undifferentiated through our resting in unity." On the surface this unknowing seems no different from Moses' entering the darkness in the *Mystical Theology*. Both terminate in unity, and both require a transcendence of thought. When Dionysius, however, says that we must "abandon thought," he means the transcendence of all thought, while the scholiast means only the transcendence of the kind of thought that scatters and gathers. Unknowing, for the scholiast, is still a form of thought. We can see this more clearly in another of the *Divine Names* scholia devoted to the subject of unknowing.[46] After calling thought a "scattering of the mind," the scholiast recommends going beyond thought. He explains what he means: "when the mind becomes whole and turns to what is inside it, becoming oneness and simplicity, it will be able to take in the divine rays through a praiseworthy unknowing." Unknowing here occurs when the mind becomes whole, not being divided into thoughts, and when it turns to what is inside it, rather than what is outside. The turning to what is inside it is, of course, the characteristic of the Plotinian universal mind in its activity of knowing. Returning to the former scholium, we find that there too the scholiast characterizes unknowing as the mind's turning to what is inside it. He says: "we do not unknow like the unlearned, who know from something other than themselves, and so become able to learn what until then they did not know." The unlearned, who possess only ignorance, the first kind of unknowing, seek knowledge outside themselves. If such a person were ignorant about God, he would seek a book or another person to give him knowledge about God. Such knowing would have the form of scattering and gathering, and so would preclude the unknowing which allows true knowledge of God.

---

[46] *PG* 4: 264.1. See Appendix B.

In the scholia on the *Mystical Theology*, we find several instances of this cognitive orientation. When Dionysius advises Timothy to abandon all things by a "surpassing" or "ecstasy," the scholiast carefully limits the extent of this surpassing.[47] For Dionysius, it means going beyond everything sensible and intelligible, including one's own mind. The scholiast eliminates this last stage, defining "surpassing" only as "the stepping back from every relation." The mind must not address itself to what is outside it, so as to have a relation with it, for relation requires at least two terms, and this multiplication would be a departure from the simplicity of the mind. The mind must step back even from relation to itself. It must be conscious, but not self-conscious. Another scholium, on Moses' entering the darkness, in one line transforms this act from union into cognition.[48] The scholiast tells us that after Moses was united to the unknown, "he then knew everything by unknowing." The union whose object was for Dionysius the over-being alone now includes all things, and is no longer union but knowledge. The mind which communes with God by simplifying itself is then able to know all things from the divine perspective.

The fruit of this extraordinary knowledge is a humility in our ordinary knowledge of the over-being. From the third kind of unknowing described by the scholiast, we descend to the second kind, the form of knowledge which knows that the unknowable cannot be known. The scholiast says: "when we turn back again from this silence in speechlessness, and descend from muteness to utterance, and understand that we unknew, we draw back from seeking everything else about the unknowable." The experience of unknowing is an antidote to a restless curiosity which seeks total discursive knowledge of God. It demonstrates that God is truly to be known only by a different means than the discursive.

In the Greek scholiasts on Dionysius we find the first representatives of the intellectual tradition, which resolves union with God into a form of knowing. Alhough Eriugena likely never read the Greek scholia, either in Greek or in their Latin translation, his translation of Dionysius continues this tradition.

ERIUGENA'S TRANSLATION OF THE MYSTICAL THEOLOGY

We must distinguish Eriugena's initial reading of Dionysius, as translator, from his later reading as composer of the *Periphyseon*. Eriugena was likely coming across Dionysius for the first time when he translated it for Charles the Bald. His translation reflected his attempt to grapple with the unfamiliar style of Dionysius. He does not

---

[47] *PG* 4: 417.4 (p. 59, below).
[48] *PG* 4: 421.1 (p. 67, below).

seem to have been completely satisfied with the first few works he translated. The manuscript tradition reveals a large set of variant readings cobbled between the lines of the *Heavenly Hierarchy* and the *Ecclesiastical Hierarchy*, the first two works that Eriugena translated.[49] These variants, possibly inserted by Eriugena himself, are more idiomatic and more accurate than the original translations. Later works, like the *Mystical Theology*, have fewer variants, reflecting Eriugena's growing ability to achieve a satisfactory translation on his first pass through the text. After he completed his Dionysius translation, he went on to write his own major work, the *Periphyseon*, which remained devoted to the Augustinian and Origenian influences of his earlier work, but showed a more profound understanding of Dionysius. The *Periphyseon* radically emphasizes the non-cognitive character of the divine being and the unknowing that unites us to it, while the Dionysius translation tends to reduce this union to a form of knowing.

Eriugena's translation of the *Mystical Theology* differs in a number of passages from the modern critical edition of the Greek text. We face a difficulty in trying to determine whether Eriugena made these changes, or whether they had already crept into the Greek manuscript he was using. Eriugena made his translation of Dionysius from the same venerable manuscript used by Hilduin. The manuscript — *Paris, Bibl. Nat., Gr. 437* — still exists, but it no longer contains the *Mystical Theology*. Our only guides to the version of the *Mystical Theology* contained in that manuscript are now the translations of Hilduin and Eriugena. With this in mind, I have adopted the following method of determining whether a variation from the critical Greek text is Eriugena's own or whether it was already present in his Greek manuscript: if Hilduin's translation matches the critical edition, while Eriugena's differs, then I conclude that the variation was made by Eriugena himself. If Hilduin and Eriugena both present the same variation, then I tentatively conclude that it was present in the Greek. I say tentatively, because Eriugena had Hilduin's translation available to him as he worked. If he looked to Hilduin for guidance in translating difficult passages, he may have followed Hilduin's mistake, without that mistake being present in the Greek. Despite this difficulty, the general tone of Eriugena's translation is clear. He follows the intellectual tradition in Dionysius interpretation, toning down the distinction between thought and union in the mystical ascent to the extent that they may be conceived as a single act.

Perhaps the most well known of Eriugena's departures from the Greek is his translation of the Greek term "beyond" (ἐπέκεινα) with the Latin "summit" (*summitas*).[50] This important change has the effect of blurring thought and union. Dionysius characterizes

---

[49] Cf. H. F. Dondaine, *Le corpus dionysien*, 42–50. The variants take into account Eriugena's later reflection on the Dionysian corpus in his *Expositions on the Heavenly Hierarchy*, and so must postdate that work.
[50] R. Roques discusses this translation briefly in *Libres sentiers vers l'érigénisme* (Rome: Edizioni dell'Ateneo, 1975), 117–9.

the summit as the highest point of being. It has the character of being, since it belongs to the same "mountain," as it were, as all other beings. The soul can go further than this summit, and press on into "the darkness where, as the discourses say, the one beyond all things truly is."[51] The darkness is not part of the mountain, but over it. It does not have the character of being, then, but is beyond it. Eriugena translates this same passage as "the darkness, where, as the discourses say, the summit of all things truly is." The entry into the darkness no longer goes beyond the mountain of being, but only reaches its highest point, a point already occupied by a form of thought. The union in the darkness now occupies the same place as the highest form of thought. The *summitas* translation is not the first case where Eriugena departs from the Greek to reduce the soul's union to its thought. When he translates "onrush," the term used by Plotinus and Dionysius to characterize the non-cognitive interaction with the divine ray, Eriugena renders it once as "viewpoint" (*speculatio*), and once as "contemplation" (*theoria*).[52] He renders the non-cognitive Greek term in cognitive Latin terms, and so eliminates the distinction between union and thought.

Eriugena also makes a number of changes to the structure of the Greek text, most of which have this same effect. First, he reads the Greek "then" (τότε) as "that" (ὅτι) in the first chapter of the *Mystical Theology*.[53] Dionysius is following Plotinus, and the account of Moses in Exodus for that matter, in using temporal language to distinguish the soul's union, typified by Moses' entry into the darkness, from its thought, typified by his contemplation of the place where God stood. First, Moses contemplates the place of God. Dionysius says, "I think this means that the summits of things seen and thought are certain underlying structures of things subordinate to the one who transcends all." After describing these underlying structures, Dionysius returns to the account of Moses' ascent: "and then, he is freed even from things seen and seeing." The term "then" separates Moses' contemplation of the place from his entry into the darkness. When Eriugena changes the "then" to "that," he changes the structure of the passage. The clauses that in Greek describe the entry into the darkness are now simply additional descriptions of Moses' contemplation of the place. When the descriptions of the place are taken together with the descriptions of the entry, they read: "I think this means that the summits of things seen and thought are certain underlying structures of things subordinate to the one who transcends all ... and that he is freed even from things seen and seeing." The elements of Moses' entry into the darkness now belong to his contemplation of the place where God stood.

---

[51] *MT* 143, 16–7 (1000C).
[52] *PL* 122: 1116C; 1135A.
[53] See below, p. 69.

Eriugena also makes several changes to the Greek description of the unknowing that takes place in the darkness. Dionysius says that Moses "renounces all the awarenesses of insight." Eriugena reads the Greek "renounces" (from ἀπόμνυμι) as "teaches" (from ἀπομυέω).[54] Instead of abandoning intellectual awareness, Moses now participates in its characteristic act, the act of teaching. Hilduin also reads the Greek "renounces" as "teaches," and so the manuscript he and Eriugena shared may itself have read "teaches," the result of an intellectualization of unknowing already performed by a Greek scribe. A little later, Eriugena alone eliminates the only use of the important term "union" in the entire *Mystical Theology*. At the close of the first chapter, Dionysius says that Moses is "united for the better to what is wholly unknown, by the inactivity of all his insight." Eriugena reads the Greek "united" (ἐνούμενος) as "than thought" (νούμενου), and so he changes "united for the better" to "what is better than thought."[55] With this simple change, the important Dionysian and Neoplatonic concept of a union transcending thought drops out of the *Mystical Theology*.

Eriugena makes one further change to Dionysius' account of unknowing. In the last line of the first chapter, Dionysius says that Moses was in a state of "knowing beyond intellect by knowing nothing." Eriugena reads the Greek "knowing" (γινώσκων) as "of those who know" (γινωσκόντων), and so he translates the line as "we must know nothing over the soul of those who know like this."[56] Dionysius uses the confrontation of "knowing" and "beyond intellect" to suggest that Moses is not knowing in any recognizable way, having surpassed his power of knowing. Eriugena's revision of the line eliminates this confrontation. The line no longer describes Moses' experience of self-transcendence, but suggests that we must follow Moses' form of knowing in order to achieve this final state.

Even if we take these changes together with Eriugena's idiosyncratic translation of "summit," we do not find in them a radical new philosophy unheard of in Dionysius. In the opening lines of the *Mystical Theology*, Dionysius himself prays to be guided to the "loftiest peak of the mystical discourses," where mysteries of theology are cloaked "in an over-shining darkness." Dionysius here does not radically separate the peak from the darkness. He goes on to say that this is the darkness of a "silence that teaches in secret." Eriugena and Hilduin's apparent introduction of teaching to the experience of the darkness at the end of the first chapter only repeats what Dionysius himself has already said. Eriugena's changes simply curb the more radical distinction between knowing and union at the end of the first chapter, eliminating the tension Dionysius

---

[54] See below, p. 69.
[55] See below, p. 71.
[56] See below, p. 71.

develops there in favor of an intellectual encounter with the over-being which incorporates the mystical into itself.

ANASTASIUS' TRANSLATION OF THE GREEK SCHOLIA

Anastasius, the papal librarian, read Eriugena's translation with a mixture of admiration and dismay. At least, this is what Anastasius told Charles the Bald in a letter written to accompany the return of Eriugena's translation from Rome to the Frankish court. Anastasius told Charles that he marveled that an Irishman — "that barbarian, placed at the ends of the earth" — could perform such a feat of translation.[57] He lamented, however, that Eriugena had produced such a literal translation, using a "word-for-word" method rather than a "meaning-for-meaning" method. Anastasius did not set aside Eriugena's translation because of this failure. Quite the contrary. He took a step that would ensure the primacy of Eriugena's translation by adding to it his own translation of the Greek scholia on Dionysius.[58]

Although Anastasius' letter criticizes Eriugena for adopting a word-for-word style of translation, and claims that Anastasius himself will adopt a freer meaning-for-meaning style of translation, he is no less literal than Eriugena in his translation of the scholia. Occasionally this fidelity to the form of the Greek text results in awkward Latin constructions, as when Anastasius retains the Greek genitive absolute, rather than turning it into a Latin ablative absolute.[59] While his translation of the *Mystical Theology* scholia never has to face Greek genitive absolutes, Anastasius at times does remain faithful to the Greek to the detriment of his Latin. For instance, take one case where the Greek reads ἐκ τοῦ δευτέρου τῆς ἀφαιρέσεως ("we begin from the secondary privation"). The Greek preposition ἐκ takes a noun in the genitive case. Its Latin counterpart, *ex*, takes a noun in the ablative case. Anastasius changes δευτέρου from the genitive to the

---

[57] Anastasius' letter can be found in *PL* 122: 1025–9.
[58] Anastasius may have been serving his own ends when doing Eriugena this favor. Recent scholarship suggests that Anastasius' program of translating Greek texts was intended to put the Latin church on an equal theological footing with Byzantium. See G. Arnaldi, "Anastasio Bibliotecario," in *Dizionario Biografico degli Italiani* 3 (1961), 25–37; C. Leonardi, "L'agiografia romana del secolo IX," in *Hagiographie, cultures et sociétés, IVᵉ-XIIᵉ siècles* (Paris: Études Augustiniennes, 1981), 471–89; "Anastasio bibliotecario e le traduzioni dal greco nella Roma altomedievale," in *The Sacred Nectar of the Greeks*, ed. M. W. Herren and S. A. Brown (London: University of London, 1988), 277–96; B. Neil, *Anastasius Bibliothecarius' Latin Translation of Greek Documents Pertaining to the Life of Maximus the Confessor* (Ann Arbor: UMI, 1998), 38–40.
[59] For example, at *PG* 4: 221.1 (24), the genitive absolute φωνῆς μεγάλης γενομένης becomes the inexplicably genitive *vocis factae* in Anastasius' translation.

ablative case in his translation, so that it makes sense behind the preposition *ex*, but he leaves the following word, ἀφαιρέσεως, in the genitive case out of faithfulness to the Greek, resulting in the awkward Latin formulation *ex secundo privationis* ("from the second of privation").[60] Recent scholarship has noted that this excessive literalism, combined with the explicit claim that he has avoided literal translation, is characteristic of all Anastasius' translations from the Greek.[61]

Anastasius' translation of the Greek scholia does have one great virtue. He did not have to rely on the same Greek manuscript as Hilduin and Eriugena. By consulting Greek manuscripts of Dionysius already circulating in Rome, manuscripts better than the one at Saint-Denis, Anastasius was able to correct some of Eriugena's departures from the Greek. Some of Anastasius' corrections take the form of new scholia, written in the margin of Eriugena's translation together with the Greek scholia. For instance, when Eriugena translates the Greek ἀμύστων ("uninitiated") as *ardentibus* ("firebrands"), Anastasius adds his own scholium by way of correction: "where the translator puts 'firebrands,' the Greek has 'unimbued' or 'uninitiated' — that is, 'unhallowed.'"[62] Other Anastasian corrections appear in the text itself, above the word or phrase they correct. By the thirteenth century, other authors had made their own contributions to these interlinear corrections, providing a comprehensive critical evaluation of Eriugena's translation which was to be extremely helpful to medieval authors wrestling with Eriugena's text. Some of these corrections restore the original Greek meaning where Eriugena has modified it. For instance, where Eriugena reads the Greek "united" as "than thought," an interlinear comment notes: "the other texts have 'united.'"[63] The later interlinear commentators often take the step from mere correction to interpretation, providing a more accessible rendering of Dionysius' obscure terminology. For instance, above the Dionysian term "shadow," the reader finds "incomprehensibility"; above "discourses," the reader finds "scriptures"; above "darkness," the reader finds "inaccessible light"; above "mystery," the reader finds "secret." The interlinear comments also reduce the more obscure terms "rejection" and "clearing off" to "denial," and the terms "selection" and "setting down" to "affirmation." The thirteenth-century reader came to the text of the *Mystical Theology* with much of the interpretive work already done for him, finding difficult metaphors and foreign concepts set within a more familiar Latin framework.

---

[60] See below, p. 91.
[61] See B. Neil, *Anastasius Bibliothecarius' Latin Translation*, 83.
[62] See below, p. 63.
[63] See below, p. 71.

THE *PERIPHYSEON* EXCERPTS

In selecting excerpts for his edition of the *Mystical Theology*, the thirteenth-century editor sought primarily those passages where Eriugena mentions Dionysius by name. As a result, the excerpts are neither a complete survey of Eriugena's treatment of mystical theology, nor are they necessarily the best passages that could have been chosen. Only two of the excerpts deal at all with the nature of mystical union.[64] Neither one mentions the important theme of the *reditus specialis*, the union of the elect with God, which is Eriugena's most important acknowledgement of a union that transcends all thought. Also, since the editor selected his excerpts almost entirely from the *Periphyseon*, they do not reflect Eriugena's later exploration of mystical union in works like the homily on the prologue to John's gospel, and the commentary on John's gospel itself.

The thirteenth-century editor chose instead to focus on Eriugena's exploration of the *Mystical Theology*'s affirmative and negative theology. Eight of the twenty-one excerpts deal with the nature of such theology, while most of the rest are applications of it to specific names: denying, for instance, that "imagination," "number," and "virtue" can be predicated properly of God. The editor drew the eight excerpts that deal with the nature of theology from the first book of the *Periphyseon*, where they can be found within a few lines of each other. In these excerpts, Eriugena explains that the affirmation "God is" and the negation "God is not" do not contradict each other. He takes "God is not" to be literally true, while "God is" must be read metaphorically. When we say "God is truth," we do not "properly affirm that the divine substance is truth, but that it can be called by such a name through a crossing (*metafora*) from creature to creator."[65] He has earlier stated the axiom which makes such metaphors possible: "what causes can reasonably be signified through the means of causality."[66] Eriugena here weakens affirmative theology considerably, by restricting its literal application to God's causality and denying that it can speak of God himself. Eriugena then applies this method to those terms with the prefix "over-," such as "over-being" and "over-god."[67] These terms seem to give us a third form of signification, different from either affirmation or denial. They provide an affirmation in saying that God is "being" and "god," yet they also provide a denial in saying that he is "over" being as we know it, and "over" god as we know him. Eriugena acknowledges that these terms contain in themselves

---

[64] *PP* IV.42.8–26 (p. 57, below) and II.136.24–138.13 (p. 109, below). The *Periphyseon* is quoted from Eriugena, *Periphyseon*, ed. I. P. Sheldon-Williams and É. Jeauneau (Dublin: Dublin Institute for Advanced Studies, 1968–).
[65] *PP* I.80.20–82.12 (p. 81, below).
[66] *PP* I.72.33–74.13 (p. 81, below).
[67] *PP* I.84.1–14 (p. 53, below).

both the affirmative and negative form of theology, but he goes on to say that the two forms of theology are present in them in different ways. These terms "possess the form of the affirmative part in their articulation, but the power of the ban in their meaning." When we use them, we cannot help but make an affirmation, since they do not contain a negation. Yet if we look beneath the surface, we find that the meaning of the term is indeed negative. The term "over-being" does not "say what God is, but what God is not. For it says that God is not being, but more than being." The meaning of terms with the "over-" prefix is then the same as the meaning of negative terms. The role of affirmative theology in them has been reduced to the mere form of the words.

Eriugena explains why affirmations such as "God is truth" cannot literally be predicated of God: there are other names opposed to them.[68] "Goodness," for instance, is opposed to "badness," and "truth" is opposed to "falsehood." As it is with names, so it is with the things they signify. Goodness has an opposite, as does truth. For this reason, their names "cannot properly be predicated of God, to whom nothing is opposed." God can have no opposite, and so the divine names, which do all have opposites, cannot properly be predicated of him. As a result, we add the "over-" prefix when predicating divine names of God: "God, then, is called 'being,' but that is not properly 'being' to which nothing is opposed. He is then *hyperousios* — that is, 'over-being.'" Eriugena makes the same argument for the name "God."[69] He derives the Greek name "God" (θεός) from the Greek verbs "to see" (θεωρέω) and "to run" (θέω). Since blindness is opposed to seeing, and not-running to running, neither term can literally describe God. We must use the term "over-god" to describe him, since he is "more than seeing" and "more than running." Here, too, Eriugena employs the prefix "over-" as a negation.

Eriugena's interpretation of affirmative and negative theology has a dramatic effect on the Dionysian forms of theology. Dionysius understands only the names drawn from the symbolic theology as metaphors. Their application to God requires that they be divorced from their ordinary signification and attached to an intelligible meaning. The divine names, on the other hand, are more intimately connected with God. They do not need to be attached to a foreign meaning, but only to be unfolded in such a way that they elevate the reader to the threshold of the silence which lies beyond them. Eriugena eliminates the Dionysian method of unfolding, and renders every name a metaphor when applied to God. "Being" is no more a proper name for God than "mixing bowl." This interpretation of the Dionysian system of naming God is peculiar to Eriugena. The Greek scholia on the *Divine Names* do once interpret the "over-" prefix as equivalent to "non-" as Eriugena does,[70] but they carefully restrict the meaning of

---

[68] *PP* I.76.16–33 (p. 53, below).
[69] *PP* I.76.35–78.9 (p. 55, below).
[70] *PG* 4: 216.1. See Appendix B.

the "non-" prefix when it is applied to names of God.[71] God "has immortality, ungraspability, unknowability, and things of this sort, not as though he were not their opposite." The prefix "non-" ordinarily designates one member of an opposed pair. "Nonmortal," for instance, designates the opposite of "mortal." God cannot have an opposite, so he must possess both the meaning of "non-mortal" and its opposite, "mortal." Eriugena, too, begins with the claim that God can have no opposite, but as we have seen, he comes to a different conclusion. Eriugena concludes that God cannot be the content meant by the positive names, the ones without the "non-" or "over-" prefix. The scholiasts conclude that God is the content meant by the names, but not in the same way as a creature would be the content meant by the names. A creature could not possess opposed contents. It could not be both "being" and "non-being." God, on the other hand, must possess both contents. Otherwise, he would have an opposite.

In the *Mystical Theology*, the Greek scholia apply this conclusion to Dionysius' claim that God is "neither shadows nor light, nor error, nor truth."[72] The scholiast here begins with the principle that God is not one of those things that are in relation with something. The kind of light we see, for instance, is in relation with darkness. Light emerges from darkness, as darkness can emerge from light. Each is potentially the other. The scholiast says that God "does not change into light from darkness, as though he changes from light in potency to light in act." This does not mean that God is not light and darkness. He is both, but in such a way that one is not opposed to the other. The opposed qualities of light and darkness "travel from him in the manner of foresight, and are second to him, or after him." Such an interpretation comes no closer to Dionysius than Eriugena's does. For Dionysius, the silence of the over-being transcends every name. For the scholiast, divine names such as "light" do apply to God, but not in the way in which they apply to creatures. When we unify our conception of the name, we rise from contemplation of light in creatures to contemplation of light itself, and finally to the silence of light as God, different from the light we see, yet tied to it through their common name.

Eriugena's more radical attribution of unknowability to God arises from a line of thought he plays out in the *Periphyseon*: that God's being is unknowable, and so worthy of negative theology, because being itself is unknowable. Any being is unknowable at heart, whether it is uncreated or created being. This latter claim is not quite as evident as the former. It is easy to think of God as unknowable, since we do not see him. How are we to think that the creatures we see — this oak tree, that sparrow — are unknowable? The information about them that we derive from our senses seems to provide us with clear knowledge of them. Eriugena explains the unknowability of being

---

[71] Cf. *PG* 4: 216.10, 361.2. See Appendix B.
[72] *PG* 4: 429.3 (58–65), p. 111, below, commenting on *MT* 150, 4–5 (1048A).

in a passage from the *Periphyseon* that the thirteenth-century editor excerpted as a commentary on Dionysius' claim: "there is neither a word for it."[73] Eriugena explains that we can ask the question "what is it?" and so acquire knowledge only of finite beings. In other words, the oak tree must be finite if I am to acquire knowledge of it. Eriugena goes on to say that beings are finite only in their circumstances, not in their substance. These circumstances are nine of Aristotle's ten categories: place, time, quantity, quality, relation, junction, state, motion, and disposition. If beings are only finite in their circumstances, then we can only know their circumstances, not their substances. I can know the place of the oak tree outside my window: it is outside my window. I can know its qualities: the green of its leaves, the roughness of its bark, and so on. None of these allow me to answer the question "what is it?" of its substance. The circumstances of the oak tree reveal that there is a substance, but they tell me nothing else about it. The same goes for God. His creation reveals that he exists, but it tells us nothing that would give us knowledge of his substance.

Substances are unknowable not because our power of knowing is weak, but because their very nature is outside the scope of knowledge. As a result, God is no more able to answer the question "what is it?" than we are when the question is asked of a substance. God does not know creatures in their substance and, more strikingly, he does not know his own substance. The thirteenth-century editor provides an excerpt from the *Periphyseon* on this latter conclusion as a commentary on the Dionysian claim that the over-being has no "understanding."[74] Eriugena explains that God "does not know in himself what he is not." One of the things that God is not is a "something" or a "what," since everything that is a "something" or a "what" has a definition. If God were to have a definition, then he would not be infinite. Since he is infinite, and so cannot be defined, then he is not a "what," and so does not know "what" he is. God may have a knowledge of created circumstances that far surpasses our own, since he sees from the creative perspective, and not the created perspective, but he is no more able to know his substance than we are.

The restriction of knowledge to circumstances, and the denial of it to substance, go beyond what Dionysius himself says. For Dionysius, substance, in the sense of *ousia* or "being," is knowable. When I see the tree outside my window and can say things about it, I am knowing the "being" of the tree. The "being" in the tree, however, can also serve as a ladder to lead me outside of sensuous particulars, and to approach the threshold of the over-being. Eriugena begins to render problematic the ladder that the intelligible names provide. The idea of a radically unknowable substance developed in his

---

[73] *PP* II.136.24–138.13 (p. 109, below).
[74] *PP* II.142.35–144.16 (p. 109, below).

Periphyseon was not to prove popular among his immediate successors, but, on the edge
of the Renaissance, it found a new exponent in Nicholas of Cusa.

NOTES ON THE PRESENT EDITION

In the present edition of the *Mystical Theology* I have tried to preserve the thirteenth-
century editor's approach to his manuscript. He did not think of it as divided into text,
footnotes, and commentary, each attributed to a single author and given its own hierarchically organized place on the page. The anonymous addition of scholia and interlinear comments, as well as the confusion of authorship over time in the case of scholia with originally known authorship, prevented the editor from identifying
contributors to the manuscript. He probably did know that the *Periphyseon*, which he
himself read and excerpted, was the work of Eriugena. In this case, the editor might
have intentionally withheld the author's name. Eriugena's own works had long been
subject to suspicion and condemnation, if not in all of Western Europe, at least in
Paris, where the editor seems to have done his work. In the end, the thirteenth-century
edition of the *Mystical Theology* mentioned by name only Dionysius, its author, and
Eriugena, its translator. The scholia then presented themselves not as the work of an
identifiable author, but as the reaction of an entire culture to Dionysius, a reaction
which took shape over seven hundred years. I have tried to preserve this presentation of
the scholia, and so have not explicitly identified their authors in the text. I have, however, identified the source of each scholium, where possible, in the margin. A reference
to *PP* indicates that the source is Eriugena's *Periphyseon; PG 4* indicates Anastasius'
translation of the Greek scholia; *PL* 122 indicates Eriugena's letter to Charles the Bald
introducing his translation of the Dionysian corpus; *PL* 106 indicates Hilduin's *Passion
of St. Dionysius; Exp.* indicates Eriugena's *Expositions on the Heavenly Hierarchy.*
    When organizing his manuscript, the thirteenth-century editor took the important
step of introducing the formerly marginal scholia into the body of the text. Many manuscripts in this tradition give the scholia the same size and lettering as the text they
comment on. All of the manuscripts in this tradition break up Eriugena's translation
into small islands of text surrounded by scholia. The primary reason for this is simply
that, with the addition of the *Periphyseon* excerpts, the scholia are much greater in
length than Eriugena's translation, but the effect is to make Eriugena's translation difficult to read in isolation. The eye of the reader moves naturally from translation to scholia. This insistent nature of the commentary had always been present in the interlinear
commentaries, which collected between the lines of Eriugena's translation even in the
earlier tradition. Some of these commentaries help the reader to make sense of Eriugena's less felicitous translations, but most of them attempt to clarify Dionysius

himself. Where Dionysius uses the suggestive term "darkness," the reader must also read above it: "that is, incomprehensibility." The interlinear commentary allows, or even compels, the reader to avoid confronting the difficulty of Dionysius' metaphoric language. I have tried, as much as possible, to preserve these disturbances of the text by the commentary. I locate the interlinear commentaries below the block of text from which they derive. Before each commentary, I have provided the word over which the commentary appears in the manuscript. As for the scholia, I have allowed them to disturb the flow of Eriugena's translation in much the way that they do in the thirteenth-century edition. The thirteenth-century editor placed a brief line of text at the beginning of most of the scholia, so that the reader might know the passage from Dionysius to which the scholium applies. At a certain point, however, he ceased to do this, and the scholia toward the end of the *Mystical Theology* are left without explicit attachment to the text. As this omission occurs in all the manuscripts, I have reproduced it here. I have indicated the absence of this line of text by placing a long dash at the beginning of such scholia. As for the relative size of the various components of the text, I have tried to reproduce the look of manuscript *Paris, Bibliothèque nationale, lat. 17341*, which uses three different styles of text: one for the title of each chapter and for headings in the preface (for which I have used a large, italicized text), one for the preface and Eriugena's translation (for which I have used a large, plain text), and one for the scholia (for which I have used a smaller, plain text). I have used italics elsewhere only to indicate the brief line of text which introduces each scholum, biblical quotations, Latin transliterations of Greek and Hebrew words, and titles of written works. The thirteenth-century editor treats the title of the third chapter as though it were itself a small chapter, and I have reproduced this as well. *Paris, Bibl. nat., lat. 17341* also identifies the author of individual scholia on the *Heavenly Hierarchy* by placing abbreviations at their head, such as "MAX" for scholia thought to be authored by Maximus the Confessor. These ascriptions, however, do not continue into other works, such as the *Mystical Theology*, and so the reader should not expect to find them here.

A large number of manuscripts contains the earlier tradition of Eriugena's translation annotated with Anastasius' translation of the Greek scholia. A comparable number contains the later tradition, the thirteenth-century edition with the excerpts from Eriugena's *Periphyseon*. I have not attempted to provide an exhaustive critical edition, which takes all extant manuscripts into account, but to provide a solid text and translation based on the best manuscripts. H. F. Dondaine, in *Le corpus dionysien de l'université de Paris au XIIIᵉ siècle*, provides a list of thirteen manuscripts containing variations of the thirteenth-century edition, seven of which include the *Mystical Theology*.[75] My own search of databases at the Institut de Recherche et d'Histoire des Textes and the Hill

[75] Dondaine, *Le corpus dionysien*, 72–3.

Monastic Manuscript Library turned up no additional manuscripts from the thirteenth-century edition. In order to select the best of these manuscripts, I compared
their readings to three sources, ranked in decreasing order of importance: (1) the earlier tradition of the Anastasian scholia, especially as found in *Paris, Bibliothèque
nationale, lat. 1618* (*A*); (2) the Greek scholia as found in Migne's *Patrologia Graeca*,
vol. 4; (3) the critical edition of Eriugena's *Periphyseon* produced by I. P. Sheldon-
Williams and É. Jeauneau.[76] I selected two manuscripts, based on their exceptional
fidelity to these three sources, from which to produce the Latin text and scholia of the
Mystical Theology:

> MS. *Paris, Bibliotheque nationale, lat. 17341* (*C*). The manuscript dates from the thir-
> teenth century, and comes from the Dominican convent of Saint-Jacques. Its contents are
> as follows. Folios 1–4v: introductory material, including Hilduin's preface to the
> Dionysian corpus, Anastasius the Librarian's letter to Charles the Bald of March 23, 875,
> verses of Eriugena, and Eriugena's letter to Charles the Bald introducing his translation.
> Folios 5–159: *On the Heavenly Hierarchy* in Eriugena's translation, with verses by Eriu-
> gena, prologues by Hugh of St. Victor and John the Sarracen, the Greek scholia in Anas-
> tasius' translation, and commentaries by Eriugena, Hugh of St. Victor, and John the Sar-
> racen. Folios 161–200: *On the Ecclesiastical Hierarchy* in Eriugena's translation, with the
> Greek scholia in Anastasius' translation. Folios 200–281: *On the Divine Names* in Eriu-
> gena's translation, with the Anastasian scholia. Folios 281–288: *On the Mystical Theology*
> in Eriugena's translation, with the Anastasian scholia. Folios 288–306: the ten letters of
> Dionysius in Eriugena's translation, with the Anastasian scholia. Folio 306–306v: apoc-
> ryphal letter of Dionysius to Apollophanes. Folios 307–354: the Dionysian corpus in
> John the Sarracen's translation. Folios 355–402v: Thomas Gallus' paraphrase of the
> Dionysian corpus, with the exception of the letters, of which only the paraphrase of the
> ninth letter is included.

> MS. *Paris, Bibliotheque nationale, lat. 1619* (*D*). The manuscript dates from the thir-
> teenth century. It may have belonged to the University of Paris as early as 1275.[77] Its con-
> tents are as follows: Folios 1–2v: introductory material, including Hilduin's preface to the
> Dionysian corpus, Anastasius the Librarian's letter to Charles the Bald of March 23, 875,
> verses of Eriugena, and Eriugena's letter to Charles the Bald introducing his translation.
> Folios 2v–163: *On the Heavenly Hierarchy* in Eriugena's translation, with prologues in
> verse and prose by Eriugena, commentaries by the anonymous scholiasts, Eriugena,
> Hugh of St. Victor and John Sarracen, with prologues. Folios 164–187: *On the Ecclesias-
> tical Hierarchy* in Eriugena's translation, with the Anastasian scholia. Folios 187–247v:

---

[76] See n. 64 above.
[77] P. Chevallier suggests that this manuscript is the *liber Dionysii cum commentis* described in the University of Paris catalogue from the years 1275–1286. See *Dionysiaca*, vol. 1 (Paris: Desclée de Brouwer, 1937),
lxxvii–lxxx.

On the Divine Names in Eriugena's translation, with the Anastasian scholia. Folios 247v–254: *On the Mystical Theology* in Eriugena's translation, with the Anastasian scholia. Folios 254–268: the ten letters of Dionysius in Eriugena's translation, with the Anastasian scholia. Folio 268–268v: apocryphal letter of Dionysius to Apollophanes. Folios 269–334v: alphabetical index, composed in the fourteenth century.

In referring to these manuscripts I preserve the sigla used by Dondaine.

Before any text could be established, I had to decide how far to follow the thirteenth-century editor. This editor had in his hands an imperfect copy of Anastasius' translation, and imperfect copies of Eriugena's works. By referring to manuscripts from the earlier tradition and to the original Greek, I could produce a text of Anastasius' translation that was better than the one in the hands of the thirteenth-century editor. I could also correct the editor's copy of Eriugena's works by referring to the numerous critical editions that have recently appeared. The resulting text would have the structure of the thirteenth-century translation, but would more accurately reflect the original texts. That is, I could produce a text which never existed. So as to avoid this outcome, and to retain the content of the thirteenth-century edition, I chose to make no modifications to the editor's version of either the Anastasian scholia or the excerpts from Eriugena. Where the editor's version differs radically from the modern critical edition of the *Periphyseon*, I have noted the variant reading in the critical apparatus with the siglum *P*. Where the thirteenth-century edition differs radically from the *Versio Dionysii* presented in Migne, I have noted the variant in the apparatus with the siglum *V*.

The choice to retain the thirteenth-century editor's version of Anastasius' scholia was more difficult, because the thirteenth-century editor had a more corrupt copy of the scholia than he did of Eriugena's works. Anastasius' scholia had fared badly in their transmission from manuscript to manuscript, probably because in the earlier tradition they were crammed into the margin. There they were often nearly illegible. The thirteenth-century editor had a better-than-average copy of the scholia, but it still contained many corrupt readings. I could have reconstructed Anastasius' original text for the sake of presenting a readable translation. The thirteenth-century edition, however, is not simply a corruption of the earlier text, but also a critical development of it. Words left in Greek by Anastasius, for example, are often supplemented in the thirteenth-century edition with a Latin transliteration. Also, certain smaller scholia are either omitted or relocated as interlinear comments. Because the thirteenth-century edition contains such a critical development, I judged it more important to present it with its virtues and defects than to recover the Anastasian original. I have, however, included in the critical apparatus important points on which the later and the earlier editions differ. I have supplied the readings from the earlier tradition as they are found in MS. *Paris, Bibliothèque nationale, lat. 1618 (A)*, an eleventh-century manuscript chosen because of its authority in Dondaine, and because it contains the crucial reading *obscurissimam*, without which

one of Anastasius' early scholia departs significantly in meaning from its Greek original.[78] I have included only those readings of *A* which correspond with the Greek text of the scholia as printed in Migne in cases where the thirteenth-century edition does not correspond with the Greek. As for cases where the thirteenth-century edition omits or relocates scholia from the earlier tradition, I have relegated the omitted scholia to Appendix A, along with scholia from the Greek original printed in Migne which either Anastasius himself omitted or which postdate his translation. The scholia which became interlinear comments can be found among the rest of the interlinear comments below the lines of Eriugena's translation. In Appendix B I have provided English translations of scholia mentioned in my introduction or footnotes, but which are found in other works of Dionysius than the *Mystical Theology*.

    I have produced the Latin text on the basis of the following principles of emendation. Where manuscripts *C* and *D* differ from each other, I have chosen the reading that agrees with the best existing edition of their source text.[79] In the case of Hilduin's *Life of Dionysius*, it is the version printed in Migne's *Patrologia Latina*, vol. 106. No reliable edition of Eriugena's Dionysius translation exists, so I relied on the Greek original printed in G. Heil and A. M. Ritter's edition, compared with Hilduin's Latin translation.[80] Since Hilduin worked from the same Greek manuscript as Eriugena, his translation serves to help identify any departure of their manuscript from those presented in Suchla's edition. In the case of the *Periphyseon*, I compared *C* and *D* to the edition of Sheldon-Williams and Jeauneau. In the case of the Anastasian scholia, I used MS. *Paris, Bibl. nat., lat. 1618* of the earlier tradition, compared with the original Greek scholia printed in Migne. Where manuscripts *C* and *D* agree with each other, but disagree with their source text, while the remaining manuscripts in the thirteenth-century edition agree with the source text, I have corrected the text to agree with the remaining manuscripts. The correction is noted in the apparatus with the siglum *E*, referring to MS. *Paris, Bibl. nat., lat. 15630*, a thirteen-century manuscript from the library of Gérard d'Abbéville.[81] Though all of the remaining manuscripts contain these readings, I chose *E* because Dondaine privileges it in his study of the thirteenth-century Dionysian

---

[78] See below, p. 56.
[79] I have indicated in the apparatus only those variations between *C* and *D* which change the meaning of the text. I have not recorded variations in spelling, spelling mistakes, and, in certain cases, synonym use. The same principle governs the variations recorded for *A* and *E*.
[80] See G. Heil and A. M. Ritter, *De Coelestia Hierarchia; De Ecclesiastica Hierarchia; Mystica Theologia; Epistulae* (Berlin: de Gruyter, 1991). G. Théry has produced an edition of Hilduin's translation in *Études dionysiennes*, vol. 2 (Paris: Vrin, 1937). It also appears in P. Chevallier, *Dionysiaca*, vol. 1.
[81] It is mentioned in the 1338 catalogue of manuscripts. See L. Delisle, *Le cabinet des manuscrits de la Bibliothèque nationale*, vol. 3 (Paris: Imprimerie Nationale, 1881), 35.

corpus. I have included the reading of *E* only in cases where it corrects both *C* and *D* to a reading which follows the source text.

In my translation, I have tried to reproduce the strangeness and occasional awkwardness of Eriugena's version. Where Eriugena leaves a word in Greek, I have left it in Greek as well, adding only a footnote to explain the meaning of the word. Where Eriugena simply transliterates a Greek word into Latin, without actually translating it, I have done the same in English. For instance, the Greek θεοσόφια, which Eriugena transliterates as *theosophia*, becomes in my translation "theosophy" rather than "divine wisdom." Where a transliterated Greek word has already become common in Latin usage, I have translated the word into an English equivalent. The Greek θεωρία, for instance, is transliterated once by Anastasius as *theoria*. His contemporaries would have little trouble understanding the term, as it is already found occasionally in the scholarly Latin of his time. I have translated it into the English "contemplation." I have also tried to preserve the occasional awkwardness which results from Eriugena's fidelity to the Greek. One example is especially worthy of note: Eriugena never attempts to paraphrase Greek words containing the ὑπερ- prefix. He simply translates the Greek ὑπερ- into the Latin *super-*, with the result that he coins many new Latin words, such as *superdeus*, which must have sounded alien to his Latin readers. I follow his lead, and do not paraphrase any of Eriugena's coinages involving the prefix *super-*. I simply translate the *super-* into the English "over-," with the inevitable awkwardness that terms like "over-god" produce. Where Eriugena or Anastasius have simply misread their text, I have not corrected their misreading, but I have attempted to present their misreading in English in a way that makes grammatical sense. I have never allowed nonsense to remain mere nonsense. In such cases, I have provided a footnote to indicate how the Greek has been misread.

Finally, the manner in which I have translated certain key terms merits explanation. Eriugena uses the two Latin terms *essentia* and *existentia*, which later philosophers were to distinguish sharply in meaning. Eriugena, however, does not distinguish their meanings, but uses both to refer to an object's existence. He understands *essentia* as a derivative of *esse*, "being," and not according to its later meaning of "essence." I have accordingly translated *essentia* as "being," and *existentia* as "reality." With the exception of *ens*, variations of *esse* appear only as forms of "to be," and not "being," to avoid confusion with *essentia*. I do not intend a significant difference in meaning between these terms any more than Eriugena intended a significant difference between their Latin originals. I have translated the pair of *positio* and *ablatio* with the English "setting down" and "clearing off." At times, their use results in an awkward English sentence. I take it that the Latin *positio* and *ablatio* fared little better in the context Eriugena applies to them. The term "setting down" reproduces both the cognitive and physical senses of *positio*. To "set down" something may either mean to posit it in the mind, or to physically put

it down. Between these two meanings lies the setting down of something in writing, where there is both the cognitive act of positing an idea, and the physical act of placing words on a page. When we "set down" the over-being, we posit it as something which may then become an object of discourse, like words on a page, using settings such as "God," "being," and "life." The "clearings" are verbal acts which "clear off" the settings as obstacles. When we "clear off the stage" or "clear off the table," we remove whatever is on it, and when it has been cleared, there is nothing but the stage or table itself. Dionysius speaks in just this way about the over-being. He says that the "clearings" clear off God — that is, they reveal him in himself by a simple act of removal. Though awkward as philosophical terms, "setting down" and "clearing off" serve like Eriugena's *positio* and *ablatio* to articulate the fundamental dichotomy of Dionysius' *Mystical Theology*.

Bibliography of Selected Works

Source Texts

The authoritative Greek edition of the Dionysian corpus is B. R. Suchla, *De Divinis Nominibus* (Berlin: de Gruyter, 1990), and G. Heil and A. M. Ritter, *De Coelestia Hierarchia; De Ecclesiastica Hierarchia; Mystica Theologia; Epistulae* (Berlin: de Gruyter, 1991). Suchla has long been preparing a critical edition of the Greek scholia, but it has not yet appeared, and they can presently be found only in the edition of B. Corderius, printed in the fourth volume of J. P. Migne's *Patrologia Graeca*. Eriugena's Latin translation of the Dionysian corpus has no modern critical edition, but it can be found in P. Chevallier, *Dionysiaca* (Paris: Desclée de Brouwer, 1937), as well as in Migne's *Patrologia Latina*, vol. 122, edited by H. J. Floss. Eriugena's *Periphyseon* may be also found in Migne, but the standard edition is that begun by I. P. Sheldon-Williams and to be completed by É. Jeauneau (Dublin: Dublin Institute for Advanced Studies, 1968–). Jeauneau is also preparing a new edition of the *Periphyseon* which takes into account the many different versions produced by Eriugena and his school (Turnholt: Brepols, 1996-). There presently exists no complete edition of Anastasius' Latin version of the scholia.

Many English translations of the *Mystical Theology* exist. The most recent is Colm Luibheid's, in his *Pseudo-Dionysius: The Complete Works* (New York: Paulist Press, 1987). Translations more faithful to the Greek can be found in J. Parker, *The Works of Dionysius the Areopagite* (London: Parker, 1897); C.E. Rolt, *The Divine Names and Mystical Theology* (London: Society for the Propagation of Christian Knowledge, 1920); J. Jones, *The Divine Names and Mystical Theology* (Milwaukee: Marquette University Press, 1980). An English translation of some Greek scholia can be found in Paul Rorem and John C. Lamoreaux, *John of Scythopolis and the Dionysian Corpus: Annotating the Areopagite* (Oxford: Clarendon Press, 1998). Eriugena's *Periphyseon* has been translated by John J. O'Meara and I. P. Sheldon-Williams. Their translation can be found in the Dublin Institute for Advanced Studies edition mentioned above, as well as in a single volume (Montreal: Bellarmin; Washington: Dumbarton Oaks, 1987).

STUDIES ON DIONYSIUS' MYSTICAL THEOLOGY

The *Mystical Theology* has inspired a vast amount of commentary, both medieval and modern. The medieval commentaries of Thomas Gallus and Robert Grosseteste have been edited and translated in James McEvoy, *Mystical Theology: The Glosses by Thomas Gallus and the Commentary of Robert Grosseteste on "De Mystica Theologia,"* Dallas Medieval Texts and Translations 3 (Leuven: Peeters, 2003). Albert the Great's commentary is edited by P. Simon in the Bonn edition of Albert's works, *Alberti Magni Ordinis Praedicatorum Opera Omnia ... curavit Institutum Alberti Magni*, vol. 37: 2 (Münster: Aschendorff, 1978), and is translated by S. Tugwell in *Albert and Thomas: Selected Writings* (New York: Paulist Press, 1989). Denys the Carthusian's commentary appears in volume 16 of the *Opera Omnia* (Montreuil-sur-Mer, Tournai, Parkminster: Typis Cartusiae S.M. de Pratis, 1896–1935). Marsilio Ficino's commentary appears in the 1576 Basilea edition of his writings, reprinted by Bottega d'Erasmo (Turin, 1962). The contemporary era of debate about the *Mystical Theology* begins with Jean Vanneste, *Le mystère de Dieu* (Brussels: Desclée de Brouwer, 1959). Vanneste's book includes a number of controversial dichotomies, including the division of Dionysius' works into theological (Neoplatonic) and theurgical (Christian). His claim that the soul has an active power for union with God has been challenged in J. Rist "Mysticism and Transcendence in Later Neoplatonism," *Hermes* 92 (1964): 213–25; and A. Golitzin, *Et Introibo ad Altare Dei* (Thessalonica: Patriarchikon Idruma Paterikōn Meletōn; George Dedousis, 1994). Other recent works on Dionysius which devote a considerable amount of attention to the *Mystical Theology* include P. Rorem, *Pseudo-Dionysius: A Commentary on the Texts and an Introduction to their Influence* (New York: Oxford University Press, 1993); and Y. de Andia, *L'union à Dieu chez Denys l'Aréopagite* (Leiden: E.J. Brill, 1996).

STUDIES ON THE GREEK SCHOLIA

A small body of papers has arisen around the question of who wrote the Dionysian scholia. The seminal work is Hans Urs von Balthasar, "Das Scholienwerk des Johannes von Scythopolis," *Scholastik* 15 (1940): 16–38. Beate Regina Suchla advances and improves on von Balthasar's conclusions in a series of articles: "Die sogenannten Maximus-Scholien des Corpus Dionysiacum Areopagiticum," *Nachrichten der Akademie der Wissenschaften in Göttingen, Philologisch-historische Klasse* (1980), 3: 31–66; "Die Überlieferung des Prologs des Johannes von Skythopolis zum griechischen Corpus Dionysiacum Areopagiticum," *Nachrichten der Akademie der Wissenschaften in Göttingen, Philologisch-historische Klasse* (1984), 4: 176–88; "Eine Redaktion des griechischen Corpus

Dionysiacum Areopagiticum im Umkreis des Johannes von Skythopolis, des Verfassers von Prolog und Scholien: Ein dritter Beitrag zur Überlieferungsgeschichte des CD," in *Nachrichten der Akademie der Wissenschaften in Göttingen, Philologisch-historische Klasse* (1985), 4: 177–93. Less work has been done on the philosophy of the scholia, but see P. Rorem, "The Doctrinal Concerns of the First Dionysian Scholiast, John of Scythopolis," in *Denys l'Aréopagite et sa postérité en Orient et en Occident*, ed. Y. de Andia (Paris: Institut d'Études Augustiniennes, 1996), 187–200; W. Beierwaltes, "Johannes von Skythopolis und Plotin," in *Studia Patristica* 108 (1972), 3–7; W. Beierwaltes and R. Kannicht, "Plotin-Testimonia bei Johannes von Skythopolis," *Hermes* 96 (1968): 247–51; R. Frank, "The Use of the *Enneads* by John of Scythopolis," *Le Muséon* 100 (1987): 101–8; and B. R. Suchla, "Verteidigung eines platonischen Denkmodells einer christlichen Welt: Die philosophie- und theologiegeschichtliche Bedeutung des Scholienwerks des Johannes von Skythopolis zu den areopagitischen Traktaten," in *Nachrichten der Akademie der Wissenschaften in Göttingen, Philologisch-historische Klasse* (1995), 1: 1–28; M. Harrington, *The Problem of Paradigmatic Causality and Knowledge in Dionysius the Areopagite and His First Commentator* (Ann Arbor: UMI, 2001), 140–86. For information on Anastasius and his program of translation, see G. Arnaldi, "Anastasio Bibliotecario," in *Dizionario Biografico degli Italiani* 3 (1961), 25–37; C. Leonardi, "L'agiografia romana del secolo IX," in *Hagiographie, cultures et sociétés, IVe-XIIe siècles* (Paris: Études Augustiniennes, 1981), 471–89; "Anastasio bibliothecario e le traduzioni dal greco nella Roma altomedievale," in *The Sacred Nectar of the Greeks*, ed. M. W. Herren and S. A. Brown (London: University of London, 1988), 277–96; B. Neil, *Anastasius Bibliothecarius' Latin Translation of Greek Documents Pertaining to the Life of Maximus the Confessor* (Ann Arbor: UMI, 1998). On Anastasius' translation of the scholia, see M. Harrington, "Anastasius the Librarian's Reading of the Greek Scholia on the Pseudo-Dionysian Corpus," *Studia Patristica*, vol. 36 (Leuven: Peeters, 2001), 119–25.

STUDIES ON ERIUGENA'S DIONYSIUS TRANSLATION

On manuscript *Paris, Bibl. Nat., Gr. 437*, Hilduin's translation of it, and the early reception of Dionysius in the Latin West, see G. Théry, *Études dionysiennes*, vol. 1 (Paris: Vrin, 1932). Théry moves on from Hilduin to Eriugena in two articles: "Scot Erigène traducteur de Denys," *Bulletin du Cange* 6 (1931): 1–94; and "Scot Érigène introducteur de Denys," *The New Scholasticism* 7 (1933): 91–108. H. F. Dondaine follows the later history of Eriugena's translation, as it acquired the Anastasian scholia, interlinear comments, and the *Periphyseon* excerpts, in *Le corpus dionysien de l'université de Paris au XIIIe siècle* (Rome: Edizioni di Storia e Letteratura, 1953). On the specific character of the thirteenth-century edition, see J. McEvoy, "John Scottus Eriugena and

Thomas Gallus, Commentators on the *Mystical Theology*," in *History and Eschatology in John Scottus Eriugena and His Time*, ed. J. McEvoy and M. Dunne (Leuven: University Press, 2002), 183–202. Other work on Eriugena's translation can be found in M. Cappuyns, *Jean Scot Érigène: sa vie, son œuvre, sa pensée* (Louvain: Abbaye du Mont César, 1933), 150–61; R. Roques, *Libres sentiers vers l'érigénisme* (Rome: Edizioni dell'Ateneo, 1975); I. P. Sheldon-Williams, "Eriugena's Interpretation of the Pseudo-Dionysius," in *Studia Patristica*, ed. E. Livingstone (Berlin: Akademie-Verlag, 1975), 151–4; É. Jeauneau, "Jean Scot Érigène et le grec," in *Archivum Latinitatis Medii Aevi (Bulletin du Cange)* 41 (1979): 5–50, reprinted in the same author's *Études érigéniennes* (Paris: Études Augustiniennes, 1987), 87–132; "Pseudo-Dionysius, Gregory of Nyssa, and Maximus the Confessor in the Works of John Scottus Eriugena," in *Carolingian Essays*, ed. U.-R. Blumenthal (Washington, D.C.: Catholic University of America Press, 1983), 137–49, reprinted in *Études érigéniennes*, 175–187; J. Pépin, "Jean Scot traducteur de Denys: l'exemple de la *Lettre IX*," in *Jean Scot écrivain*, ed. G.-H. Allard (Paris: Vrin, 1986), 129–41. For a bibliography of works examining other Latin translations of Dionysius, see U. Gamba, "Commenti latini al 'De Mystica Theologia' del Ps.-Dionigi Areopagita fino al Grossatesta," *Aevum* 16 (1942), 251–7; J. de Ghellinck, *Le mouvement théologique au XIIe siècle* (Bruges: Éditions de Tempel, 1948), 97–102.

Table of Sigla

Manuscripts

Paris, Bibliothèque Nationale, lat. 1618, ff. 79v–81v	A
Paris, Bibliothèque Nationale, lat. 17341, ff. 281–288	C
Paris, Bibliothèque Nationale, lat. 1619, ff. 247v–254	D
Paris, Bibliothèque Nationale, lat. 15630, ff. 149v–158v	E

Other Sources

Periphyseon, ed. I. P. Sheldon-Williams and É. Jeauneau	P
Versio Dionysii, ed. H. J. Floss (*PL* 122)	V

Text

Quartus de mystica theologia liber quantum coartior sit caeteris in sermonibus tantum largior in sensibus. Unde et in duas maximas logicae disciplinae dividitur partes, kataphaticam plane et apophaticam — id est in esse et non esse. Ubi analytice artis regulis utitur et nos praeclarissime commovet[1] per privationem omnium quae dici seu intelligi possunt. Oportere ad veritatem quae[2] causa omnium quae ab ea et per eam et in ea et ad eam creata sunt per essentiae excellentiam recurrere. Haec capitula continet de mystica theologia sermo: quid divina caligo; quomodo oportet et uniri et hymnos referre omnium causali et super omnia; quia kataphatikai theologiae quae apophatikai; quia nihil sensibilium omnis sensibilis per excellentiam causalis; quia nihil intelligibilium omnis intelligibilis per excellentiam causalis. Epigramma in beatum Dionysium in capitula[3] de mystica theologia: novam claritatem in reliqua et scientiam subsistentium, noctem per divinam quam non iustam licet nominare. Eiusdem ad Timotheum episcopum de mystica theologia. Compresbytero Timotheo Dionysius presbyter.

Epitoma beato Timotheo capitulatim composuit magnus areopagita Dionysius de mystica theologia per kataphasin — id est affirmationem — et per apophasin — id est negationem — atque per hypotheticos — id est conditionales — syllogismos. Omnia sensibilia et intelligibilia et quae in terra sunt et quae in caelo sensu transcendens ac prout mortali possibile est atque licitum usque ad ipsius divinitatis sacrarium penetrans. Quapropter a Graecorum sapientibus ex tunc hodieque[4] Dionysius πτερυγιον του ουργανου quod latinus sermo explicat ala[5] caeli vocatur quia illuc spirituali intelligentia et reverentissimae revelationis gratia evolans non solum illa multimoda et magnifica mysteria ac ministeria sanctorum spirituum verum et sempiternae divinitatis[6] saporem palato cordis degustans didicit. Unde haec humanae notitiae latius eructavit, in cuius libri capitulo primo dicit intimatum sibi a beato Bartholomeo apostolo qualiter theologiam sanctam quia et evangelium debuerit intelligere. Quod et argute cepit et brevibus sed profundissimis verbis eiusdem apostoli scriptis suis ea inserendo diffinivit.

---

[1] commovet] commonet *D*
[2] quae] est *V*
[3] capitula] hoc *D*
[4] hodieque] hodie quia *C*
[5] ala] *correxi ex E*, aula *C D*
[6] divinitatis] deitatis *C*

The fourth book, *On Mystical Theology*, is more compressed than the *PL* 122:1035A–1036A rest in its speech as it is broader in its meaning. For this reason, it is divided into the two greatest parts of the discipline of logic, namely the kataphatic and the apophatic — that is, into what is and what is not. There it uses the rules of the analytic art, and moves us with great clarity through the privation of everything that can be said or thought. We must retreat to the truth which, through the excellence of its being, is the cause of all the things that have been created from it, through it, in it, and for it. *The work* On Mystical Theology *contains these chapters*: what the divine darkness is; how we must be united and return hymns to the one who causes all and is over all; what the kataphatic and apophatic theologies are; that what causes everything sensuous is, through its excellence, not something sensuous; that what causes everything intelligible is, through its excellence, not something intelligible. *An epigram to the blessed Dionysius on his chapters concerning mystical theology*: "an understanding of the subsistences, and a new enlightenment on everything else, through the divine night which cannot be justly named." *From the same author to Bishop Timothy:* On Mystical Theology. *Dionysius the Elder to Timothy his fellow Elder.*

———. The great Dionysius the Areopagite composed for the blessed Timothy *PL* 106: 31C–32A this brief summary of mystical theology through *kataphasis* — that is, affirmation — and through *apophasis* — that is, denial — and through hypothetical — that is, conditional — syllogisms. His intuition transcends everything sensuous and intelligible and the contents of earth and heaven. So far as a mortal can and may, he penetrates to the shrine of the divinity itself. For this reason, Dionysius is called by Greeks then and now the πτερύγιον τοῦ οὐρανοῦ, which the Latin speech explains is the "wing of heaven." He is called this because his teaching does not merely fly out from here by his spiritual intelligence and the grace of the most reverent unveiling; it also tastes the flavor of the sempiternal divinity with the palate of the heart. Because of this, he has cast these matters out more openly for human notice. In the first chapter of his book he says what the blessed Bartholomew the apostle suggested to him as to how we ought to think of holy theology and the gospel. He grasped this acutely, and defined it with few but deep words of the same apostle, including them in his own writings.

Primi capituli titulus est quid divina caligo

The title of the first chapter is: "what the divine darkness is"

Trinitas superessentialis, et superdeus, et superoptime Christianorum inspector theosophiae, dirige nos in mysticorum eloquiorum super-incognitum et superlucentem et sublimissimum verticem,

Inspector — id est cognitor et approbator. Theosophiae — id est divinae sapientiae. Mysticorum eloquiorum — id est arcanorum verborum sacrae scripturae.

Trinitas. Superessentialis natura causa est et creatrix existentium et non existentium omnium, a nullo creata, unum principium, una origo, unus et universalis universorum fons, a nullo manans, dum ab eo manant omnia, trinitas coessentialis in tribus personis, anarchos — id est sine principio — principium et finis, una bonitas, deus unus, omoysios et yperoysios — id est coessentialis et superessentialis.[7] Et, ut ait sanctus Epiphanius, episcopus Constantiae Cypri, in sermone de fide: "tria consancta,[8] tria coagentia, tria conformantia, tria cooperantia, tria consubsistentia sibi invicem coexistentia. Trinitas haec sancta vocatur, tria existentia una consonantia, una deitas eiusdem essentiae, eiusdem virtutis, eiusdem subsistentiae, similia similiter aequalitatem gratiae operantur patris et filii et spiritus sancti. Quomodo autem sunt ipsis relinquitur docere: *nemo enim novit patrem nisi filius, neque filium nisi pater, et cuicumque filius revelaverit.* Revelatur autem per spiritum sanctum. Non ergo haec tria existentia aut ex ipso per ipsum aut ad ipsum in unoquoque digne intelliguntur nisi sicut de ipsa revelant: φως, πυρ, pneuma, hoc est lux, ignis, spiritus? Haec, ut dixi, a sancto Epiphanio tradita sunt, ut quisquis interrogatus quae tria et quid unum in sancta trinitate debeat credere, sana fide respondere valeat aut ad fidem accedens sic erudiatur. Et mihi videtur spiritum pro calore posuisse, quasi dixisset in similitudine: lux, ignis, calor. Haec enim tria unius essentiae sunt. Sed cur lucem primo dixit non est mirum. Nam et pater lux est et ignis et calor, et filius est lux et ignis et calor, et spiritus sanctus lux, ignis, et calor. Illuminat enim pater, illuminat filius, illuminat spiritus sanctus. Ex ipsis enim omnis scientia et sapientia donatur. Urit pater, urit filius, urit spiritus sanctus, quia simul nostra delicta consumunt, et nos velut holocaustum quoddam[9] theosin — id est deificationem — in unitatem suam convertunt. Calificat pater, calificat filius, calificat spiritus sanctus quia uno eodemque caritatis aestu et[10] nos fovent et nutriunt, ac veluti ex informitate quadam imperfectionis nostrae post primi hominis lapsum *in virum perfectum in plenitudinem aetatis Christi* educant. Vir autem perfectus Christus est, in quo omnia consummata sunt, cuius aetatis plenitudo est consummatio

---

[7] et superessentialis] *om. C*
[8] consancta] conscientia *D*
[9] quoddam] per *add. P*
[10] et] *om. C*

Trinity, over-being and over-god, who over-ideally look into the theosophy of Christians, guide us to the over-unknown, the over-shining: the loftiest peak of the mystical discourses.

Look into — that is, know and approve. Theosophy — that is, divine wisdom. Mystical discourses — that is, the arcane words of sacred scripture.

Trinity. The nature over being is the cause and creator of all realities and unrealities, while it is created by none. One principle, one source, one universal font of all things — it streams from nothing, while all things stream from it, the trinity sharing being in three persons. It is ἄναρχος — that is, without beginning. It is beginning and end, one goodness, one God, ὁμοούσιος and ὑπερούσιος — that is, sharing being and over being. As St. Epiphanius, the bishop of Constantia in Cyprus, says in his speech on faith: "three sharing holiness, three sharing action, three sharing form, three sharing activity, three sharing substance, three sharing reality with each other. This holy one is called 'trinity': three realities, one harmony, one deity of the same being, the same power, the same subsistence. The likeness of the Father, Son, and Holy Spirit likewise enacts an equality of grace. Now we must leave to them the teaching of what they are, *for no one knows the Father save the Son, and no one knows the Son save the Father and anyone to whom the Son has unveiled himself.*[1] Now he is unveiled through the Holy Spirit. These three realities: φῶς, πῦρ, πνεῦμα — that is, light, fire, spirit — are they not then worthily thought to be in each of the three from itself, through itself, and for itself?"[2] As I have said, these words have been handed down by St. Epiphanius, so that anyone who is asked what he ought to believe about "three" and "one" in the holy Trinity may be able to answer with a healthy faith. Or else he may receive such instruction when he comes to faith. It seems to me that St. Epiphanius put "spirit" for "warmth," as though he said, thinking of their likeness: "light," "fire," "warmth," for these three are one in being. But it is no wonder that he said light first, for the Father is light, fire and warmth; the Son is light, fire and warmth; and the Spirit is light, fire and warmth. For the Father illuminates, the Son illuminates, and the Holy Spirit illuminates, because all understanding and wisdom is given by them. The Father burns, the Son burns, and the Holy Spirit burns, because they consume our faults at once, and we, like a kind of sacrifice, return our θέωσις — that is, deification — to their unity.[3] The Father warms, the Son warms, and the Holy Spirit warms, because they tend and nourish us by one and the same wave of charity. They lead us out, as though from the so-called formlessness of our imperfection after the fall of the first human, *into the perfect man, into the fulness of the age of Christ.*[4] Now Christ, in whom all things have their fulfillment, is the perfect man. The fulness of his age is the fulfillment of the

PP IV.2.4–4.11

salutis universalis ecclesiae quae in angelis et hominibus constituta est. Merito ab hac superoptima et superessentiali trinitate in contemplationem supercaelestium rogat se dirigi magnus areopagita Dionysius.

Superessentialis. Haec nomina quae adiectione super vel plusquam particularum de deo praedicantur ut est superessentialis, superdeus, superoptimus, plusquam veritas, plusquam sapientia et similia, duarum theologiae partium — id est affirmative et negative — in se plenissime sint[11] comprehensiva, ita ut in pronunciatione affirmativae formam. In intellectu vero virtutem abdicativae obtineant. Et hoc brevi concludamus exemplo: essentia est, affirmatio. Essentia non est, abdicatio. Superessentialis est, affirmatio simul et abdicatio. In superficie etenim negatione caret, in intellectu negatione pollet. Nam quae dicit superessentialis est non quid[12] est dicit sed quid non est. Dicit enim essentiam non esse sed plusquam essentiam. Quid autem illud est quod plusquam essentia est non exprimit, deum non esse asserens aliquod eorum quae sunt sed plusquam ea quae sunt esse. Illud autem esse quid sit nullo modo diffinit.

Item. Si haec divina nomina, essentia, bonitas, veritas, iustitia, sapientia, caeteraque id[13] genus opposita e regione sibi alia nomina respiciunt, necessario etiam res quae proprie eis significantur oppositas sibi contrarietates obtinere intelliguntur, ac per hoc de deo, cui nihil oppositum aut cum quo coaeternaliter natura differens nihil inspicitur, proprie praedicari non possunt. Praedictorum enim nominum aliorumque sibi similium nullum vera ratio reperire potest cui non ex adversa parte aut secum in eodem genere differens aliud ab ipso discedens nomen non reperiatur. Et quod in nominibus cognoscimus, necessarium ut in his rebus quae ab eis significantur cognoscamus. Sed quoniam divinae significationes quae in sancta scriptura a creatura ad creatorem translate de deo praedicantur si tamen recte dicitur de eo aliquid posse praedicari innumerabiles sunt et parvitate nostrae ratiocinationis nec inveniri nec insimul colligi possunt. Pauca tamen exempli gratia divina vocabula ponenda sunt. Essentia ergo dicitur deus sed proprie essentia non est cui opponitur nihil. Yperoysios ergo est — id est superessentialis.

Superdeus. Primum de isto nomine quod est deus quod in sancta scriptura usitatissimum est considerandum arbitror. Quamvis enim multis nominibus divina natura denominetur, ut est bonitas, essentia, veritas, caeteraque huius modi. Frequentissime tamen eo nomine divina utitur scriptura. Huius itaque nominis etymologia a Graecis assumpta est, aut a verbo quod est theoro, hoc est video, dirivatur, aut ex verbo theo, hoc est curro, aut quod probabilius est quia unus

---

[11] sint] sunt *D*

[12] non quid] numquid *D*

[13] id] scilicet *C*

salvation of the universal church which has been established in angels and humans. With reason, the great Dionysius the Areopagite asks that he be guided by this over-ideal and over-being trinity in his contemplation of the over-heavens.

Over-being. Those names that are predicated of God by the addition of the pre- *PP* I.84.1–14
fixes "over" or "more than" — as that he is "over-being," "over-god," "over-ideal,"
"more than truth," "more than wisdom," and the like — these fully grasp in
themselves the two parts of theology — that is, the affirmative part and the negative part. As a result, they possess the form of the affirmative part in their articulation, but the power of the ban in their meaning. Let me close with this brief
example: "he is being:" affirmation; "he is not being:" ban; "he is over-being:"
affirmation and ban at once. Although on the surface it lacks a denial, in meaning it has the force of a denial. For when he says "he is over-being," he does not
say what God is, but what God is not. For he says that God is not being, but
more than being. Now he does not explain what that is which is more than being
when he claims that God is not one of the things that are but is more than the
things that are, and he does not in any way use his claim to define what God is.

On the same topic. If these divine names — "being," "goodness," "truth," "justice," *PP* I.76.16–33
"wisdom," and the rest of that kind — reflect other names directly opposed to
them, then we must think that the things they properly signify possess contraries
opposed to them. For this reason, they cannot properly be predicated of God, to
whom nothing is opposed, or with whom we see nothing sharing eternity but different in nature. For true reason can discover none of the aforesaid names and
others like them from which another name, departing from it, is not discovered,
either opposed to it or differing within the same class. And what we know in
names we necessarily know in those things that they signify. But although the
divine significations predicated of God in Holy Scripture — ferrying us from
creature to creator — are numberless and can neither be found nor gathered
together by our little train of thought — if we are right to say that anything can
be predicated of him — we ought, nevertheless, to posit a few divine terms for the
sake of example. God, then, is called "being," but that is not properly "being" to
which nothing is opposed. He is then ὑπερούσιος — that is, "over-being."

Over-god. First, I think we ought to consider the name "God," which is the name *PP* I.60.10–23
that Holy Scripture uses most. For although the divine nature is named with
many names — as it is "goodness," "being," "truth," and the rest of that sort —
the divine scripture still uses this name the most frequently. The Greeks have

idemque intellectus inest ab utroque dirivari recte accipitur. Nam cum a verbo theoro deducitur theos videns interpretatur. Ipse enim omnia quae sunt in se ipso videt dum nihil extra se ipsum aspiciat quia nihil extra se ipsum est. Cum vero a verbo theo theos currens recte intelligitur. Ipse enim in omnia currit et nullo modo stat sed omnia currendo implet, sicut scriptum est: *velociter currit sermo eius*. Attamen nullo modo movetur. De deo siquidem verissime dicitur motus stabilis et status mobilis. Stat enim in se ipso incommutabiliter numquam naturalem suam stabilitatem deserens. Movet autem se ipsum per omnia ut sint ea quae essentialiter subsistunt. Motu enim ipsius omnia fiunt. Ac per hoc unus idemque intellectus est in duabus interpretationibus huius nominis quod est deus. Non enim aliud est deo currere per omnia quam videre omnia, sed sicut videndo ita et currendo fiunt omnia. Deus ergo currens dicitur non quia extra se currat qui semper in se ipso immutabiliter stat qui omnia implet, sed quia omnia currere facit ex non existentibus in existentia.

Item. Deus dicitur sed non proprie deus est. Visioni enim caecitas opponitur et videnti non videns. Igitur ypertheos — id est plus quam videns — est, si theos videns interpretatur. Sed si ad aliam originem huius nominis recurras, ita ut non a verbo theoro — id est video — sed a[14] verbo theo — id est curro — theon — id est deum — dirivari intelligas, adest tibi similiter eadem ratio. Nam currenti non currens opponitur sicut tarditas celeritati. Erit igitur ypertheos — id est plus quam currens — sicut scriptum est: *velociter currit sermo eius*. Nam hoc de deo verbo, quod ineffabiliter per omnia quae sunt ut sint currit, intelligimus.

Theosophiae. Theosophia divina est sapientia quae in fidei, spei et caritatis tenore consistit. Haec est enim vera et salutifera a[15] superoptima et superessentiali trinitate summae gratis donata Christianis sapientia. De fide namque dicit apostolus: *gratis salvi facti estis per fidem, et hoc non ex vobis. Dei enim donum est*. De spe psalmista: *memento verbi tui servo tuo in quo mihi spem dedisti*. De caritate item apostolus: *caritas Dei diffusa est in cordibus nostris per spiritum sanctum qui datus est nobis*. Haec est proprie[16] verorum Christianorum sapientia. Hic est sors[17] eorum proprius cui non communicat alienus.

---

[14] a] *om. C*
[15] a] et *C*
[16] proprie] propria *add. D*
[17] sors] fons *D*

undertaken the etymology of this name. It is derived either from the word θεωρέω — that is, "I see" — or from the word θέω — that is, "I run" — or we may rightly take it to be derived from both. This is the more likely, since their meaning is one and the same. For since θεός is drawn from the word θεωρέω, it is translated "seeing." For he sees all the things that are in him, while he looks at nothing outside himself, since outside him there is nothing. But since θεός is from the word θέω, it is rightly thought of as "running," for he runs into all things. In no way does he rest, but he fills all things by running, as we find it written: *his speech runs swiftly.*[5] But still, in no way does he move. Of course, a resting motion and a mobile rest are truly said of God, for he rests changelessly in himself, never abandoning his natural restfulness. Now he moves himself through all things, so that those that subsist in the manner of being may be, for all things come about by his motion. For this reason, there is one and the same meaning in the two translations of the name "God." For God's running through all things is none other than his seeing all things, yet as by his seeing, so by his running, all things come about. God, then, is called "running" not because he runs outside himself, who always rests changelessly in himself, and fills all things. Rather, it is because he makes all things run from unreality into reality.

On the same topic. He is called "God" but he is not properly God, for blindness is   *PP* I.76.35–78.9
opposed to vision and not-seeing to seeing. He is then ὑπέρθεος — that is, "more than seeing," if "God" is translated as "seeing." But if you go back to the other origin of this name, so that you think θεός — that is, "God" — is derived not from the word θεωρέω — that is, "to see" — but from the word θέω — that is, "to run" — the same structure will still be present to you. For "not running" is opposed to "running," as "slowness" is to "speed." He will then be ὑπέρθεος — that is, "more than running" — as we find it written: *his speech runs swiftly.* For we think this refers to God the Word, because he indescribably runs through all the things that are so that they may be.

Theosophy. Divine theosophy is the wisdom which lasts as long as faith, hope, and   ?
charity. For this wisdom is given to Christians by the grace of the true, preserving, over-ideal, and over-being highest Trinity. For about faith the Apostle says: *You have been saved by grace and through faith. This is not of you, for it is the gift of God.*[6] About hope the Psalmist says: *remember your word to your servant, through which you have given me hope.*[7] About charity, again the Apostle says: *the charity of God has been poured into our hearts through the Holy Spirit who was given to us.*[8] This is properly the wisdom of true Christians. This is their proper lot, in which no one else shares.

ubi nova et absoluta et inconversibilia theologiae mysteria, secundum superlucentem absconduntur occulte docentis silentii caliginem, in obscurissimo, quod est supermanifestissimum, supersplendentem,

Absoluta — id est pura et sine figuris. Inconversibilia — id est invariabilia. Theologiae — id est scripturae de deo loquentis. Mysteria — id est secreta. Docentis — iuxta illud *audiam quid loquitur in me dominus deus.*

Ubi nova. Nova sive simpla seu simplicia et absoluta dicit quae sine symbolis intelliguntur et aspiciuntur ut se habent, non tamen parabolice.

Et absoluta. Absoluta dixit — id est quae non secundum apertionem nominum vel symbolorum dicuntur, sed absolutione quae ex omnibus intelligibilibus est, necnon et intelligentiarum cessatione collecta, quam ut quandam otiositatem intellectualis motus in antecedentibus quidem insipientiam vocavit. Hic autem obscurissimum et invisibile.[18]

Caliginem. Nubes et caligo in circuitu eius. Et: *posuit tenebras latibulum suum.*

et in qua omne relucet, et invisibilium superbonorum splendoribus superimplentem invisibiles intellectus.

Intellectus — id est angelos.

Intellectus. Non enim sensibilibus oculis sunt pleni, sed est eorum essentia, intellectus tota oculus acutissimus utpote vivens. Unde et multorum oculorum esse dicuntur in oratione.

Mihi quidem haec opto. Tu autem, o amice Timothee, circa mysticas speculationes corroborato itinere et sensus desere, et intellectuales operationes, et sensibilia, et invisibilia, et omne non ens, et ens;

Mysticas — id est arcanas. Speculationes — contemplationes.

Et sensus desere. Non enim aliter conditori suo adhaerere posset mens humana si omnia quae sub ipsa sunt et seipsam non excederet, quoniam "inter mentem nostram," ut ait Augustinus, "qua patrem intelligimus et veritatem per quam ipsum intelligimus nulla interposita creatura est." Quod etiam ipse areopagita,

---

[18] obscurissimum et invisibile] obscurissimam <caliginem> et invisibile<m> *A*

New, free and unbending mysteries of theology are cloaked there in
the over-shining darkness of a silence that teaches in secret.

Free — that is, pure and without shape. Unbending — that is, unvarying. Mysteries — that is, secrets. Theology — that is, scripture, when it speaks about God.
Teaches — as in: *let me hear what the Lord God speaks in me.*[9]

New. He calls "new" or "simple" or "simplified" and "free" what we think of and
look at as it is, without symbols and parables.

Free. He calls "free" the mysteries that are not spoken in names or symbols, but
gathered by our freedom from all that is intelligible, and undoubtedly by the cessation of our thoughts. In his earlier works he called this "lack of wisdom," since it is
a kind of idleness of the intellectual motion. Here he calls it "mistiest and unseen."[10]

Darkness. Cloud and darkness are on his track.[11] And: *he has made the shadows his
refuge.*[12]

PG 4: 416.7 (1–3)

PG 4: 416.7 (3–9)

PG 4: 416.7 (9–11)

The darkness, in which everything shines out, over-beams the greatest over-revelation in the greatest mist. It more than fills the unseen
intellects with the beams of unseen over-goods.

Intellects — that is, angels.

Intellects. For their eyes are not filled with the sensuous, but their being is wholly
intellect — a supremely sharp and living eye. For that reason they are also called
"many eyed" in the prayer.[13]

PG 4: 417.1

I want these things for myself. As for you, Timothy, my friend — take the
paved path around the mystical viewpoints. Abandon the senses, intellectual activities, the sensuous, the unseen, every non-being and every being.

Mystical — that is, arcane. Viewpoints — contemplations.

Abandon the senses. For if the human mind did not surpass itself and everything
under it, it could not otherwise cling to its founder, since, as Augustine says, "no
creature is set between our mind by which we think of the Father, and the truth
through which we think of him."[14] The Areopagite himself, Dionysius, I mean,
teaches this beautifully in his *Mystical Theology.* He says: "Timothy, my friend,"
and so on. And in the gospel the Lord says: *where I am, there is also my minister.*[15] Now the Lord is over all things. The human who clings to him is then over
all things and over himself, inasmuch as he is in all things. Although human

PP IV.42.8–26

Dionysium[19] dico, in mystica theologia pulchre docet dicens: "O amice Timothee," et caetera. Et in evangelio dominus ait: *ubi ego sum illic et minister meus.*
Est autem ille super omnia. Est[20] igitur illi adhaerens homo super omnia et super
seipsum, quantum in omnibus est. Et quamvis humana natura, dum in hac vita
mortali versatur, adhaerere deo re ipsa non possit, verumtamen, quoniam possibile est ei et naturale[21] conditori suo adhaerere eius gratia cui adhaeret, adhaerere
in imagine dicitur. Saepe enim possibilitas pro experimento solet accipi et quod
certum est quandoque fore pro praesenti computari et etiam pro peracto.
Et sensibilia. Ex quo[22] idipsum indicatur. Sensibilia quippe ipsa vocant veteres
non existentia, ut omnis commutationis participantia, et non similiter semper
manentia. Intelligibilia vero, ut semper immortalia voluntate factoris et non
essentiam suam semper mutantia, existentia dicunt, ut saepe diximus.

> et ad unitatem, ut possibile, inscius restituere ipsius, qui est super
> omnem essentiam et scientiam. Ea enim teipso et omnibus immen-
> surabili et absoluto pure mentis excessu ad superessentialem div-
> inarum tenebrarum radium, omnia deserens et ab omnibus absolu-
> tus ascendes.[23]

Unitatem — id est simplicitatem et super omnem unalitatem. Inscius — aut
ignote. Teipso — a teipso. Omnibus — ab omnibus. Immensurabili — Graecus
irretento. Divinarum tenebrarum — id est divinae incomprehensibilitatis.

Inscius. Quomodo inscie sive ignote restituatur sive extendatur quis ad deum et
nos quidem in capitulo quinto de divinis nominibus prosecuti sumus, et hic post
pauca invenies.
Immensurabili. Certum est quod immensurabilem sive irretentibilem excessum
dixerit recessum ab omni affectu sive habitudine, ut nullo possideatur affectu,
nec eo qui ad se ipsam est, multo amplius vero nec eo qui est ad[24] aliquid creat-
urarum.
Tenebrarum. Et hic tenebras omnimodam incomprehensibilitatem ait.

---

[19] Dionysium] Dionysius *D*
[20] Est] Erit *D*
[21] naturale] naturali *C*
[22] quo] equo *D*
[23] ascendes] ascendens *D*
[24] qui est ad] quid est ad *C*

nature, while wound up in this mortal life, cannot cling to God in fact, it is nevertheless said to cling in his image, since it is also possible for it to cling to its natural founder by the grace of the one to whom it clings. For possibility is customarily taken for experience, and what is certain to come someday is customarily put for present and even for accomplished.

The sensuous. Which indicates the same thing. The ancients especially called the   *PG* 4:417.2
sensuous "unreality," since it participates in all kinds of change and does not always remain alike. Now they called intelligibles "realities," as I have often said, since, by their maker's will, they are immortal and do not always change their being.

Restore yourself without understanding, so far as you can, to unity with what is itself over all being and understanding. For when you abandon all things and are freed from all things, you will ascend to the divine shadows' ray over being by a purely free surpassing of the mind,[16] which cannot be measured by it, you, or anything.

Without understanding — that is, unknowingly. Unity — that is, simplicity over even all union. Divine shadows' — that is, divine incomprehensibility's. Cannot be measured — the Greek has "cannot be held up." You — by you. Anything — by anything.

Without understanding. I followed out how one is restored or extended to God   *PG* 4: 417.3 (2–4)
without understanding or unknowingly in the fifth chapter of *On the Divine Names*, and here you will find it a little later.[17]

Which cannot be measured. No doubt he calls "surpassing which cannot be mea-   *PG* 4: 417.4
sured" or "held up" the stepping back from every attitude or character, so that no attitude may possess it, neither toward itself, nor, all the more, toward any creature.

Shadows. Here too, he calls "shadows" what cannot be grasped in any way.   *PG* 4: 417.5

His autem, vide, quomodo nemo indoctorum auscultet. Indoctos autem dico in his quae sunt conformatos, et nihil supra existentia superessentialiter esse imaginantes. Sed his quidem hi, quos videre ea, quae secundum seipsos est, scientia oportet tenebras latibulum eius.

Quomodo — id est ut. In his — in sensibilibus. Existentia — id est haec visibilia. His — id est inter istos. Hi — sunt. Scientia oportet — id est qui oportere iudicant. Tenebras — id est incomprehensibilitatem.

Indoctorum. Notandum quod indoctos dicat eos etiam qui non sunt mysticorum inexpertes, sensibilibus tamen infixos, et nil super existentia esse imaginantes. Denique de universalibus indoctis mox prosecutus ait.

Secundum ipsos. Id est qui existimant talem esse deum sicut intelligere valent.

Si autem super hos sunt divinae in mysteria introductiones, quid quis dixerit de aliis ardentibus, quicunque omnibus superpositam causam ex ipsis in his quae sunt novissimis characterizant, et nihil eam superare aiunt ab ipsis fictarum impietatum et multiformium formationum?

In mysteria — id est in arcana sacrae scripturae. In his — id est quae sunt in existentibus. Characterizant — id est signunt vel figurant. Multiformium — idolatras describit et publicat evidenter.

Super hos. Fideles scilicet qui in corruptibilibus sunt conformati sive intenti.

Item. Hos ait qui crediderunt quidem Christo,[25] non tamen ad perfectiorem processerunt scientiam, sed commensurant scientia sua veritatem, nescientes existentium proprie et non proprie existentium sed omonime existentium — id est[26] essentiarum et accidentium differentiam, et ipsius super existentia existentis, ac per hoc et[27] superessentialis. Huiusmodi ergo ut indocti sublimiorum arbitrantur in veritate tenebras esse obscuram hanc adumbrationem quae tegat deum et abscondat eum ab omnium visione, quod revera intelligunt multi et in nobis, utpote non cognoscentes excellentissimam lucem omnem vultum obtenebrantem. Si ergo et inter nos tales, quid putas dicemus super idololatris qui penitus sunt omnium mysticorum inexpertes?

---

[25] Christo] Christum *A*
[26] id est] *om. A*
[27] et] *om. C*

See how no one untaught overhears these matters. Now by untaught I mean: "conformed to the things that are," and "imagining that nothing is over realities in a manner over being." As for them — those[18] that must use their own kind of understanding to see — *shadows are his refuge.*[19]

How — that is, that. To the things that are — to the sensuous. Realities — that is, these visible things. As for them — that is, among them. Those — there are those. That must — that is, who think they must. *Shadows* — that is, incomprehensibility.

Untaught. Note that he also calls "untaught" those who are not inexperienced in the mysteries, but who are attached to the sensuous, and who imagine there is nothing above realities. He soon follows this up, speaking finally about the entirely untaught. *PG* 4: 417.6 (1–5)

Their own kind. That is, those who deem that God is such as they are able to think. ?

If the divine introductions to the mysteries are over their heads, what will we say about the other firebrands: those who characterize the cause set over all things with the very last of all the things that are, and say that it overcomes none of their contrived treacheries and manifold formations?

Mysteries — that is, the arcana of sacred scripture. The things that are — that is, that are in realities. Manifold — he plainly describes and proclaims the idolaters.

Over their heads. The faithful, you understand, who are conformed to or held up by things that decay. *PG* 4: 417.7 (17–8)

On the same topic. He speaks of those who believed in Christ, but did not *PG* 4: 417.7 (1–15)
proceed to a more perfect understanding. They measured out the truth by their understanding, and did not understand the difference between realities proper and realities not proper but by equivocation, between beings, accidents, and the very reality over realities, which for this reason is also over being. This sort of person, then, untaught in loftier matters, thinks that the shadows are really a misty outline that covers God and cloaks him from the sight of all. Many, even among us, actually think this, in that they do not know of the most excellent light which shadows every countenance. If there are such even among us, what do you suppose we should say about the idolaters, who are thoroughly inexperienced in all that is mystical?

Ardentibus. Ardentes quod interpres posuit Graecus non imbutos seu initiatos — id est non consecratos — habet. Et notandum quod alios indoctos dicat et alios non imbutos.

> In ipsa etiam oportet omnes existentium ponere et affirmare positiones, veluti omnium causa, et omnes eas potentius negare, tanquam super omnia superexistente, et non aestimari depulsiones oppositas esse intentionibus, sed multo prius ipsam super privationes esse, quae est super omnem ablationem et positionem.
>
> Depulsiones — id est negationes. Intentionibus — id est affirmationibus. Ablationem — id est negationem. Positionem — id est affirmationem.

In ipsa. Ut[28] omnia existente deo decenter, et nihil existente superessentialiter. Ipsa enim et positio est et depulsio, nam et proprie utraeque super divina dicuntur magnitudine.

Et affirmare. Quid sint affirmationes seu intentiones positionum et depulsiones ablationum, et quid privationes, et hic quidem disseritur, et maxime in tertio capitulo, et in hoc qui de divinis nominibus sermone diverse ac late interposuimus.

Et omnes. Nam[29] videtur his qui philosophantur quod depulsiones oppositae sint affirmationibus, sed non in divina essentia hoc sit. Super omnem enim est deus et ablationem et positionem. Lege[30] in sermone qui est de caelesti hierarchia.

> Sic igitur divinus Bartholomaeus ait et multam theologiam esse, et minimam, et evangelium latum, et magnum, et iterum correptum. Mihi videtur supernaturaliter intelligens quia et multiloqua est optima omnium causa, et breviloqua simul, et sine verbo, quomodo neque verbum, neque intelligentiam habet, eo quod omnibus ipsa superessentialiter superposita est,
>
> Bartholomeus — apostolus scilicet. Multam — id est multarum dictionum. Minimam — id est paucorum verborum.

---

[28] Ut] Et *D*
[29] Nam] *correxi ex E,* Iam *C D*
[30] Lege] et *add. A*

Firebrands. Where the translator puts "firebrands," the Greek has "unimbued" or "uninitiated" — that is, "unhallowed." Note that Dionysius calls some "untaught" and others "unimbued."

Anast.
PG 4: 417.6 (5–7)

We must also set down and affirm the setting of realities in it as the cause of all things. With greater might, we must deny them all, since it over-exists over all things. We must not judge that the rejections oppose the selections, but that the one who is over all clearing off and setting down is himself already over the privations.

Rejections — that is, denials. Selections — that is, affirmations. Clearing off — that is, denial. Setting down — that is, affirmation.

In it. Since it is all things in a manner suited to God and is nothing, in a manner over being. For it is both setting down and rejection — both are said properly of the divine greatness.

PG 4: 417.8 (1–4)

And affirm. Here, and most of all in the third chapter, he discusses what the "affirmations" or "selections" of the settings are, and what the "rejections" of the clearings are, and what the privations are. I, too, have set them down in a broad and varied manner in the work entitled *On the Divine Names.*[20]

PG 4: 417.8 (4–8)

All. For it seems to those who philosophize that the rejections oppose the affirmations. But this is not so in the divine being, for God is over both clearing off and setting down. Read this in the work entitled *On the Heavenly Hierarchy.*[21]

PG 4: 420.1 (1–4)

The divine Bartholomew, then, says that theology is both much and the least, and that the gospel is broad, large, and again, clipped. To me, he seems to understand that the ideal cause of all things says a lot and a little at once. It is without a word, since it has neither word nor intelligence, in that it has itself been set over all things in a manner over being.

Bartholomew — the apostle, you understand. Much — that is, of many statements. The least — that is, of few words.

Bartholomeus. Nota et hinc non fictum et sincero affectum sancti Dionysii has divinas conditiones exponendi. Ante haec[31] namque in aliis sermonibus memoriam fecit testimoniorum quorundam qui fuerunt[32] cum apostolis. Testimonium affert ut manifestet[33] quod ait. Si enim sine scripto esset docens dixisset utique ait. Notandum ergo quod et sanctus Bartholomeus scripsit.

Et multiloqua. Multiloqua quod Graecus πολυλογος — id est polilogos — habet si in penultimo ponatur accentus significat eum qui multum loquitur. πολυλογος vero cum in antepenultimo accentum habet indicat eum qui multis eget sermonibus vel multis depraecatur orationibus. Sicut et πρωτοτοχος — id est prototocos — si antepenultimum habet accentum significat primogenitum. Sicut[34] πρωτοτοχος accentu in penultimo posito insinuat feminam quae primogenitum peperit. Si vero [35] πρωτοτοχος penultimum habet accentum significat primogentium,[36] sicut et Homerus ostendit:

προτοτοχος χινυρη ου πριν ειδυια τοχοιο.

Neque verbum. Scilicet propriae naturae ut exhibitorum in his quae forinsecus sunt. Similiter et de intelligentia est opinandum.

> et solis incircumvelate et vere manifesta, polluta omnia et munda[37] transgredientibus, et omnem omnium sanctarum summitatum ascensionem superascendentibus, et omnia divina lumina et sonos et verba caelestia superantibus, et in caliginem occidentibus, ubi vere est, ut eloquia aiunt, omnium summitas.
>
> Incircumvelate — id est sine velamine. Polluta omnia — id est omnia sensibilia. Transgredientibus — id est vivacitate spiritualis intelligentiae. Sanctarum summitatum — scilicet angelorum. Caliginem — id est lucem inaccessibilem. Eloquia — id est in epistula Pauli ad Timotheum.

Et sonos. Sonos et verba seu sermones caelestes ait quae de deo in scriptura dicuntur, ut non secundum humanum et terrenum sensum, sed secundum divinam inspirationem dicta et tradita.

---

[31] haec] hoc *C*
[32] fuerunt] fuerant *C*
[33] manifestet] manifestat *A*
[34] Sicut] Si vero *A*
[35] Sicut] Si vero *A*
[36] Si vero πρωτοτοχος penultimum habet accentum significat primogenitum] *om. A*
[37] munda] immunda *D*

Bartholomew. From this we may also note the uncontrived and sincere attitude of *PG* 4: 420.2 (1–9)
St. Dionysius as he explains these divine circumstances. For before now he made
mention in his other works of the witness of some who were with the apostles.
He brings in a witness to reveal what he is saying.[22] For if Bartholomew were
teaching without writing, Dionysius would say at least: "says."[23] Note, then, that
even St. Bartholomew wrote something down.

Says a lot. "Says a lot," which in Greek is πολυλόγος — that is, *polilogos* — if the *PG* 4: 420.3
accent is put on the penult, it means "he who says a lot." But when πολύλογος
has its accent on the antepenult, it indicates "he who needs much speech" or
"who prays many prayers." Likewise, if πρωτότοκος — that is, *prototokos* — has
its accent on the antepenult, it means "firstborn." Likewise, if the accent of προ-
τοτόκος is put on the penult, it suggests a woman who gave birth to her firstborn. But if πρωτοτόκος has its accent on the penult, it means "firstborn,"[24] as
Homer, too, demonstrates: πρωτοτόκος κινύρη οὐ πρὶν εἰδυῖα τόκειο.

Neither word. In its own nature, you understand, as is shown by those outside *PG* 4: 420.4
our tradition. We should guess something similar about "intelligence" as well.

> It reveals itself truly and unveiledly only to those who cross from all
> things soiled and clean, who ascend over every ascent of all the holy
> summits, who overcome all the divine lights, sounds, and heavenly
> words, and who fall into the darkness where, as the discourses say,
> the summit of all things truly is.
>
> Unveiledly — that is, without a veil. Who cross from — that is, by the liveliness
> of their spiritual intelligence. All things soiled — that is, all things sensuous. Holy
> summits — the angels, you understand. Darkness — that is, inaccessible light.
> Discourses — that is, in Paul's letter to Timothy.

Sounds. He calls "sounds" and "heavenly words" or "speeches" what is said of *PG* 4: 420.5
God in scripture, since it is said and handed down not by a human and earthly
intuition, but by divine inspiration.

Etenim non simpliciter divinus ipse Moyses primus[38] mundari iube-
tur, et iterum ab his, qui tales non sunt, segregari,

Simpliciter — id est sine causa vel ratione. Tales — scilicet mundi.

Ipse Moyses. Nota ordinem eorum quae in Moysae acta sunt, antequam ingred-
eretur caliginem.

Et iterum. Enarratio dicti quod[39] est per compositionem sic intelligenda, quia Moyses, contemplatus locum ubi stabat deus, et dein absolutus ab his quae con-
spiciebantur — id est sensibilibus omnibus — atque conspicientibus — id est ratio-
nabilibus universis — tunc in caliginem introivit — id est in ignorantiam quae est
de deo — ubi, omnibus depositis cognoscibilibus auxiliis seu susceptionibus, factus
est in intractabili et invisibili loco, cunctarum cognoscibilium receptionum seu aux-
iliorum eius qui super universa est deus.[40] Et unitus per talem modum ignorantiae
et inoperationi seu inefficaciae — id est ei qui omnino est ignotus ab omni scientia
et universorum summus atque supremus — tunc ignorantia[41] omnem[42] cognovit.

et, post omnem purgationem, audit multivocas tubas, et videt luminaria multa aperte fulgurantia et multum fusos radios. Deinde multis segregatur, et cum electis sacerdotibus in summitatem divinarum
ascensionum praecurrit, et si eis sic manentibus fit Deo, contem-
platur vero non ipsum, invisibilis est enim, sed locum ubi stetit.

Multis — a multis. Et si eis sic manentibus fit deo — alia licta: et si in his cum
ipso quidem non fit deo.

Luminaria. Quod dictum est quia mons Sina incendebatur ab igne.
Locum. Quis locus in quo stetit deus tempore Moysi.

Hoc autem arbitror significare divinissima et sublimissima visibilium
et intelligibilium, hypotheticos quosdam esse sermones, subiectorum
omnia superanti, per quae super omnem intelligentiam ipsius
praesentia ostenditur, intelligibilibus summitatibus sanctissimorum
eius locorum supergrediens:

---

[38] primus] primum *C*
[39] quod] quae *C*
[40] deus] *gr.* θεοῦ
[41] ignorantia] ignorantiam *C*
[42] omnem] esse *C*

In fact, the divine Moses himself is not simply ordered first to be cleansed, and then set apart from those who are not.

Simply — that is, without cause or reason. Those — of the world, you understand.

Moses himself. Note the order of what was accomplished in Moses before he entered the darkness. *PG* 4: 420.6 (4–5)

And then. We ought to think of the composition of the story he has told as follows: that Moses contemplated the place where God stood, then he was freed from what we look at — that is, everything sensuous — and from what does the looking — that is, everything that reasons. Then he entered the darkness — that is, the unknowing which concerns God. Here he put aside all the aids or supports of knowledge, and came to be in the place of the one who is God over the universe, untouched and unseen by any reception or aid of knowledge. He was united through such a mode to unknowing and inactivity or inefficacy — that is, to the one who is altogether unknown to all understanding, and who is the highest of all and supreme. Moses then knew everything by unknowing. *PG* 4: 421.1
(1–12, 15–7)

After every purification he hears the chorus of trumpets, he sees the many luminaries openly sparkling, and the great outpouring of their rays. Then he is set apart in regard to the masses, and runs with his chosen priests to the summit of the divine ascents. If, while they remain, he comes to be with God,[25] he still does not contemplate him — for God is unseen — but the place where he has stood.

In regard to the masses — from the masses. If, while they remain, he comes to be with God — the other texts have "if, in those who were with him, he does not come to be with God."

Luminaries. Note that he says Mt. Sinai was scorched by fire. ?
Place. What the place was in which God stood when Moses came. *PG* 4: 420.7 (1–2)

Now what signifies this, I think, are certain hypothetical speeches, the most divine and loftiest of things seen, thought, and subject to the one who overcomes all. They demonstrate his presence over all intelligence, a presence which paces over the intelligible summits of his most holy places.

Hypotheticos — id est contemplatorios. Sermones — sive rationes. Subiectorum — eorum quae subiecta sunt. Superanti — id est deo. Super omnem — quae est supple. Intelligibilibus summitatibus — angelicis essentiis quae scilicet sunt loca ipsius sanctissima.

Divinissima. Quid sublimitates sive summitates intelligibilium, et quid visibilium sint, in sermone qui est de hierarchia quae in caelis est in fine primi capituli praefati sumus.

Hypotheticos. Hypotheticos sermones ait subscriptitios — id est contemplatorios existentium, quae subiecta deo esse ait. Per ipsos enim — id est per horum perseverantiam et conservationem — omnibus eum adesse docemur, non transitorie, sed provide. Intelligibiles vero sublimitates sive summitates caelestes et intellectuales essentias quae circa deum sunt vocat, quas et loca ipsa sanctissima nominavit. Super quae et ipse superpositus — id est absolutus — est nullatenus eis quoquomodo similis aestimandus.[43]

et quod ipsis absolvitur visibilibus et videntibus, et in caliginem ignorantiae occidit vere mysticam, per quam docet omnes gnosticas receptiones, et in qua omne relucet, et invisibili innascitur omnis, qui est in omnium summitate, et a nullo, neque a seipso, neque altero,

Ipsis — ab ipsis. Absolvitur — Moyses scilicet. Quam — scilicet caliginem. In omnium summitate — scilicet illius qui est super omnia. A nullo — scilicet intelligitur.

In caliginem. Notandum quod caliginem ignorantiam intellexerit.

Ignorantiae. Quomodo per ignorantiam deus cognoscitur, et in sermone qui est de divinis nominibus dictum est. Oportet autem sciri, quod in Exodo, ubi scriptum est, quia ingressus est Moyses in caliginem ubi erat deus, Hebraicum quidem habet araphel. Septuaginta vero, et Aquila, et Theodosio araphel caliginem ediderunt. Symmachus tamen nebulam araphel interpretatus est. Porro Hebreus dicit araphel nomen esse firmamenti in quod pervenerit Moyses. Septem enim firmamenta ait, quae et caelos vocant, quorum memoriam fieri nunc non est urgendum. Legi autem septem caelos et in scripta ab Aristone Pelleo disputatione Papisci et Iasonis, quam Clemens Alexandrinus in sexto libro υποτυπωσεων — id est ypotyposeen — sanctum Lucam ait scripsisse. Verum de caligine, in divinam ignorantiam conspecta, divinius philosophatus est et in epistularum suarum. Quoque quinta perfecte de hoc scribit.

---

[43] aestimandus] existimandus *D*

Hypothetical — that is, contemplative. Speeches — or structures. Subject — those that are subject. The one who overcomes — that is, God. Over all — add: "which is." Intelligible summits — the angelic beings which, you understand, are his most holy places.

Most divine. I have already said what the "loftinesses" or "summits" of the intelligible and visible things are at the end of the first chapter of his work *On the Hierarchy in the Heavens.*[26]

PG 4: 420.7 (2–5)

Hypothetical. He calls "hypothetical speeches" those that sketch out — that is, that contemplate — the realities he says are subject to God. For we learn through them — that is, through their persistence and preservation — that God is present to all things, not by crossing through them but by his foresight. Now he calls "intelligible loftinesses" or "summits" the heavenly and intellectual beings which surround God. He has also named them the "most holy places themselves." He himself is over-set — that is, freed — over them. He is in no way at all to be judged like them.

PG 4: 420.8

They also signify that[27] he is freed in regard to the very things that see and are seen, and falls into the truly mystical darkness of unknowing. He teaches[28] all the gnostic receptions through the darkness in which everything shines out. In the unseen, all of him is born, who is in the summit of all things and is from none, neither himself nor another.

He is freed — Moses, you understand. In regard to the very things — from the very things. Which — the darkness, you understand. In the summit of all things — of him who is over all things, you understand. Is from none — is thought of by none, you understand.

Into the darkness. Note that he has thought of unknowing as darkness.

PG 4: 421.1 (17–8)

Of unknowing. He has also said how God is known through unknowing in his work entitled *On the Divine Names.*[29] Now you ought to understand that in *Exodus*, where it is written that Moses entered the darkness where God was, the Hebrew has *araphel.* The *Septuagint*, though, as well as Aquila and Theodosius, have put "darkness" for *araphel.* This did not stop Symmachus from translating *araphel* as "cloud." The Hebrew, moreover, says that *araphel* is the name of the firmament Moses reached. For he says there are seven firmaments, which they also call heavens, but we do not now need to recall them. I have also read of the seven heavens in the *Debate of Papiscus and Jason*, written by Aristo Pelleus, which Clement of Alexandria, in the sixth book of his ὑπο-τυπώσεις — that is, *hypotyposeis* — says St. Luke wrote. Dionysius has truly philosophized more divinely in his letters, too, about the darkness we look at in divine unknowing. He writes about this perfectly in the fifth of these.

PG 4: 421.1 (18–37)

omnino autem ignoto omni scientia in otio per id quod melius est intellectus, et nihil cognoscendum super animum sic cognoscentium.

Ignoto — deo scilicet. Otio — id est cessante. Intellectus — alia licta unitus.

Ignoto. Notandum quia omnis scientiae otio ignoto unimur.
Et nihil. Notandum qualiter hic bene exprimat scientiam dei quae est in ignorantia.

Now it is altogether unknown to all understanding in idleness, through what is better than thought.[30] We must know nothing over the soul of those who know like this.[31]

It — God, you understand. Idleness — that is, cessation. Thought — the other texts have "united."

Unknown. Note that we are united to the unknown by the idleness of all our understanding.   *PG* 4: 421.2

Nothing. Note how well he expresses here the understanding of God which is in unknowing.   ?

Capitulum II

*Quomodo oportet uniri et hymnos referre
omnium causalis et super omnia*

Chapter II

How we must be united and return hymns
to the one who causes all and is over all

Iuxta hanc nos fieri superlucentem oramus caliginem, et per invisibilitatem et ignorantiam videre et cognoscere ipsum super Deum et
scientiam.

Deum — vel visionem quod graecus habet.

Caliginem. Et hic de divina caligine et ignorantia ait.
Ignorantiam. Notandum quia hoc est sub divina fieri caligine, per invisibilitatem et
ignorantiam videre et scire ipsum quod super visionem atque scientiam est, neque
videre neque scire. Hoc enim est ait vere videre atque scire. Nusquam autem sic edisserit scientiam quae est in ignorantia. Lege et quintam ad Dorotheum epistulam.

Hoc non videre et scire, idipsum est vere videre et cognoscere, et
superessentialem superessentialiter laudare per omnium existentium
ablationem,

Per omnium. Id est eo[44] quod omnium nihil connaturale illi excogitetur. Hoc
enim ablationem nominavit.

sicut per seipsum naturale agalma facientes, auferunt ea, quae
superadiecta sunt, pura occulti visione vetantia, et ipsam in seipsa
ablatione sola occultam manifestant formam.

Agalma — id est imaginem.

————. Per seipsum naturale agalma sive quod per se naturale simulacrum sit
ait, quod sit in materia non incisa, ut in saxo solido, dum stetit, ut et Euripides
ait in Andromeda: "virginisque imaginem quandam ex se ipsis formatis lapideis
parietibus sapientis simulacrum." Dixit quod ex saxo naturaliter ortum est. Sed
et cum partem quandam arboris sculpens stantis, lecti partem feceris, quod
Odysseus fecit ut Homerus ait. Aiunt autem et timiae lapidis simulacrum — id
est splendorem — ad quod maxime nunc intuens dixit pater, ut Dionysius poeta
in secundo[45] lapideorum: "aut spissi viroris[46] existentis iaspidis, aut amethisti
porphyriantis simulacrum, tetrum aut iacinctus." Haec autem omnia ostendunt
quam multae fuerit hic sanctus pater eruditionis.

---

[44] eo] *om. C*
[45] secundo] secunda *C*
[46] spissi viroris] *gr.* βαθυχλοάοντος

We pray to be made like this over-shining darkness, to see through unseeing and unknowing, and to know the very darkness over God[32] and understanding.

God — or "vision," as the Greek has it.

Darkness. Here, too, he speaks about divine darkness and unknowing.

PG 4: 421.3 (1–2)

Unknowing. Note that to come under the divine darkness is this: to see and understand through unseeing and unknowing that which is above sight and understanding, and neither to see nor understand it. For he says that this is both to see truly and to understand. Now he has nowhere so described the understanding which lies in unknowing. Read also his fifth letter, to Dorotheus.

PG 4: 421.3 (2–9)

Not to see and understand — this is itself to see and to know truly, to praise the over-being in a manner over being, through the clearing off of all realities.

Through the clearing off of all. That is, in that we know nothing that shares its nature, for this is what he names "clearing off."

PG 4: 421.4 (1–3)

Likewise, those who make a statue that is so by nature — they clear off the overgrowth that prevents the pure sight of the hidden. By clearing alone, they reveal the very hidden form in itself.

Statue — that is, "image."

Statue that is so by nature. He calls "statue that is so by nature" or "what is a portrait by nature" what is in uncut matter, as in solid rock, so long as it remains so. As even Euripides says in his *Andromeda*: "a sort of image, a portrait of the wise virgin, arising from the stone walls formed by themselves." He says that the image arose naturally from the rock. Then, too: when you make a part of your bed by sculpting some part of a standing tree, which Odysseus did, as Homer says. Now they also mention a portrait — that is, a beam — of *timia*[33] stone. Father Dionysius has spoken now after reflecting on these most of all, like Dionysius the poet in the second book of *Stones*: "a portrait either of the solid force of jasper, or purple amethyst, or rough sapphire." Now all these examples show how great was the learning of this holy father.

PG 4: 421.4 (3–15, 17–24)

Oportet autem, ut arbitror, ablationes in contrarium positionibus laudare. Etenim illas quidem a praestantissimis inchoantes, et per media in novissima descendentes, apponimus.

Ablationes — id est negationes in deitate. Positionibus — id est affirmationibus. Illas — scilicet affirmationes. Praestantissimis — id est excellentissimis.

Ablationes in contrarium. Quid sunt positiones et ablationes, in sermone de divinis nominibus diverso habemus modo. Item praesentem locum in subsequentibus idem pater edisserit. Siquidem positiones sunt quaecumque proprie in deo dicuntur, quia est ut puta on, vita, lux, et alia. Ablationes vero quaecumque ut aliena a deo asseruntur, ut puta quia non corpus deus, non anima, nec quicquam eorum quae cognoscuntur, aut intelligentiae submittuntur.

Hinc vero a novissimis ad principalissima[47] ascensiones facientes, omnia auferimus, ut incircumvelate cognoscamus illam ignorantiam, ab omnibus ignorantibus in omnibus existentibus circumvelatam, et superessentialem illam videamus caliginem, ab omni in existentibus luce occultatam.

A novissimis — scilicet in negationibus. Incircumvelate — scilicet sine velamine.

Hinc vero. Existentium scientiae quod de deo est ignotum non detegunt vel in manifestationem ducunt. Sed potius contegunt et abscondunt. Lumen vero in existentibus accipiendum est cognoscere existentia utrum existentia sint, quemadmodum et in sequentibus reperimus.

---

[47] principalissima] *correxi ex E*, principalissimas *C D*

Now we must, I think, praise the clearings with their opposed settings. In fact, when we set them down, we begin with the most outstanding and descend through the middle to the last of all.

Clearings — that is, the denials that concern the deity. Settings — that is, the affirmations. Them — the affirmations, you understand. The most outstanding — that is, the most excellent.

Clearings with their opposed. We hear what the settings and clearings are in a different way in his work *On the Divine Names.* Father Dionysius himself, moreover, discusses the present passage in what follows. The settings, of course, are whatever we say of God properly — for instance, that he is ὤν, life, light, and other things. Now the clearings are whatever we assert as foreign to God — for instance, that God is not a body, not a soul, nor anything that is known or that yields to intelligence. *PG* 4: 424.1

Now from here we clear off all things, making our ascent from the last of all to the chiefest, so that we may know that unknowing unveiledly — for it is veiled from every unknowing[34] reality — and so that we may see that darkness over being, hidden from all the light in realities.

From the last of all — in the denials, you understand. Unveiledly — without a veil, you understand.

Now from here. Understanding of realities does not uncover or lead to revelation what is unknown about God. It rather covers and cloaks. Now we must take the "light in realities" to know realities, whether they are realities, as we also discover in what follows. *PG* 4: 424.2

Capituli iii titulus quae sunt kataphatikai
theologiae quae apophatikai

The title of Chapter Three is:
"what the kataphatic and apophatic theologies are"

Quae sunt kataphaticae theologiae, quae apophaticae.

Kataphaticae — id est affirmativae. Apophaticae — id est negativae.

————. Duae principales theologiae partes sunt: affirmativa quidem, quae a Graecis kataphatice, et abnegativa, quae apophatice dicitur. Una quidem — id est apophatice — divinam essentiam seu substantiam esse aliquid eorum quae sunt — id est quae dici possunt aut intelligi — negat. Altera vero — id est kataphatice — omnia quae sunt de ea praedicat et ideo affirmativa dicitur, non ut firmet eam aliquid esse eorum quae sunt, sed omnia quae ab ea sunt de ea posse praedicari suadeat. Rationabiliter enim per causativa causale potest significare.[48] Dicit enim esse veritatem, bonitatem, essentiam, lucem, iustitiam, solem, stellam, spiritum, aquam, leonem, ursum, et vermem, et caetera innumerabilia. Et non solum ex his quae sunt secundum naturam eam edocet, sed ex his quae contra naturam quando eam inebriari, stultitiamque esse, et insanire dicit. Sed de his nunc sufficiat. Satis enim de talibus a sancto Dionysio areopagita in symbolica theologia dictum est.

Item. Duas sublimissimas theologiae partes esse diximus et hoc non ex nobis sed auctoritate sancti Dionysii areopagitae accipientes qui apertissime bipertitam theologiam asserit esse — id est in kataphatiken et apophaticen — quas Cicero in intentionem et repulsionem transfert. Nos autem, ut apertius vis nominum clarescat, in affirmationem et negationem maluimus transferre. Haec autem duo quae videntur inter se esse contraria nullo modo sibimet opponuntur dum circa divinam naturam versantur, sed per omnia in omnibus sibi invicem consentiunt. Et ut hoc apertius fiat paucis utamur exemplis. Verbi gratia kataphatice dicit veritas est, apophatice contradicit veritas non est. Hic videtur quaedam forma contradictionis, sed dum intentius inspicitur nulla controversia reperitur. Nam quae dicit veritas est non affirmat proprie divinam substantiam veritatem esse sed tali nomine per metaforam a creatura ad creatorem posse vocari. Nudam siquidem omnique propria significatione relictam divinam essentiam talibus vocabulis vestit. Ea vero quae dicit veritas non est merito divinam naturam incomprehensibilem ineffabilemque clare cognoscens non eam negat esse, sed veritatem nec vocari proprie nec esse. Omnibus enim significationibus quas kataphatice divinitatem induit apophatice eam spoliare non nescit. Una enim dicit sapientia est verbi gratia, eam induens. Altera dicit sapientia non est, eandem exuens. Una igitur dicit hoc vocari potest, sed non dicit hoc proprie est. Altera dicit hoc non est quamvis ex hoc appellari potest.

---

[48] significare] significari *P*

What the kataphatic and apophatic theologies are.

Kataphatic — that is, affirmative. Apophatic — that is, negative.

————. There are two chief parts of theology: the affirmative, which is called *kataphatice* by the Greeks, and the negative, which is called *apophatice*. One — that is, the *apophatice* — denies that the divine being or substance is one of the things that are — that is, that can be said or thought. But the other — that is, the *kataphatice* — predicates of it all the things that are, and so it is called "affirmative." Not that it affirms it as one of the things that are, but it suggests that all the things that are from it can be predicated of it. For it can reasonably signify what causes through the means of causality. For it says that it is "truth," "goodness," "being," "light," "justice," "the sun," "a star," "spirit," "water," "a lion," "a bear," "a worm," and numberless others. It teaches of it using not only the natural, but the unnatural, when it says that it "gets drunk," "is foolish," and "goes mad." But enough of this now. For St. Dionysius the Areopagite has said enough about such matters in his *Symbolic Theology*. *PP* I.72.33–74.13

On the same topic. We have said that the loftiest parts of theology are two. We take this not on our own authority, but that of St. Dionysius the Areopagite, who quite openly asserts that theology is bisected — that is, into the *kataphaticen* and the *apophaticen*, which Cicero translates as "selection" and "rejection." But I prefer to translate them as "affirmation" and "denial," so that the force of the names may enlighten us more openly. Now these two, which seem to be contraries, are in no way opposed to each other when they are wound up in the divine nature, but they agree with each other through and through. Let me use a few examples to open this up a little. For instance, the *kataphatice* says: "he is truth." The *apophatice* contradicts it: "he is not truth." This seems a certain form of contradiction, but when we look into it more carefully, we find nothing controversial. For the saying "he is truth" does not properly affirm that the divine substance is truth, but that it can be called by such a name through a crossing from creature to creator. He clothes the divine being with such terms, of course, though it is bare and abandoned by all proper signification. But the saying "he is not truth" worthily and plainly knows that the divine nature cannot be grasped or spoken. It does not deny that it is, but that it is properly called either "truth" or "being." It is not unaware that the *apophatice* strips the divinity of all the significations with which the *kataphatice* robes it. For one says "it is wisdom," for example, robing it. The other says "it is not wisdom," disrobing it. One then says "it can be called this," but it does not say "it properly is this." The other says "it is not this, although it can be called it." *PP* I.80.20–82.12

Capitulum III

Chapter III

In theologicis igitur characteribus potentissima affirmativae theologiae laudavimus,

————. Quid continet sermo theologicorum characterum sive doctrinarum.

quomodo divina et optima natura unica dicitur, quomodo triadica,
quae secundum ipsam dicta et[49] paternitas, et filiolitas, quid[50] vult
declarare in spiritu theologia, quomodo ex immateriali et impartibili
optimo in corde bonitatis germinata sunt lumina,
Triadica — id est trina. Optimo — scilicet deo. Lumina — scilicet filius et spiritus sanctus.

In corde bonitatis. Theologiae recte hic munimena[51] ait et orthodoxia summa repleta.
Hoc autem est scire quomodo singularis divina natura sit per id quod trium subsisten-
tiarum est, scire personarum differentiam,[52] et quae sit sancti spiritus sanctifica virtus,
quid significat: *eructavit cor meum verbum bonum*, et quomodo de spiritu sancto dictum est: *qui ex patre procedit*, et quomodo in patre et in se ipsis et in invicem, filius, et
spiritus in mansione immobili sunt. Oportet autem scire, quod mansio et statio idipsum sit, et motus secundus sit a mansione. Ait ergo quia in mansione immobili semper existens divina natura, putatur moveri in meatu qui est in invicem.

et quomodo ipsius in ipso et in seipsis et inter se invicem coaeternae
in germinatione mansionis servaverunt reditum,

Et quomodo. Hic est sensus dictorum. Coaeterna est, inquit, existentia sanctae
trinitatis, et non aliter quidem existit, et aliter[53] haec constituta est aut
separationem quandam aut transmutationem habuit, sed pariter et similiter tunc
ex patre esse filium et spiritum sanctum, et non post eum.

quomodo superessentialis Iesus humanis naturalibus veritatibus essentia
factus est, et quaecunque alia ab eloquiis expressa sunt secundum theo-

---

[49] et] *om. C*
[50] quid] ergo est hoc aut quid *add. C*
[51] munimena] monimina *A*
[52] differentiam] differentias *A*
[53] aliter] alter *C*, post *add. A*

I have, then, praised the mightiest matters of affirmative theology in my *Theological Characters*:

————. What his work on the theological characters teaches.   *PG* 4: 424.3 (1–2)

that the divine and ideal nature is called "unitary" and "triadic;" what we call "fatherhood" in itself, and "sonship;" what theology means to say in relation to the Spirit; that lights have sprouted in the heart of goodness, arising from the immaterial and partless ideal; Triadic — that is, threefold. Lights — the Son and the Holy Spirit, you understand. Ideal — God, you understand.

In the heart of goodness. He is right to speak these bulwarks of theology, filled   *PG* 4: 424.3
with the highest orthodoxy. Now this is to understand that the divine nature is   (2–5, 7–20)
single through what belongs to the three subsistences; to understand the distinction of the persons, and what the sanctifying power of the Holy Spirit is; what *my heart has discharged a good word* means;[35] how *who proceeds from the Father* is said of the Holy Spirit;[36] and how the Son and Spirit are in a motionless remaining in the Father, in themselves, and in each other. Now you must understand that remaining and rest are the same, and motion is second to remaining. He says, then, that the divine nature, which always exists in a motionless remaining, is supposed to be moved by the route of the subsistences into each other.

that in sprouting they continue to return to that shared eternal remaining in itself, in themselves, and in each other;

That. This is the meaning of what he says: he says the reality of the Holy Trinity   *PG* 4: 425.1
is eternal, and did not at one time exist and at another time establish itself or possess a sort of separation or change. Then, and not later, the Son and the Holy Spirit were equally and likewise from the Father.

that natural human truths made a being out of Jesus, who is over being; and anything else the discourses have expressed in theological

logicos characteres. In eo autem qui est de divinis nominibus, quomodo optimus nominatur, quomodo on, quomodo vita, et sapientia, et
virtus, et quaecunque alia intelligibilis sunt divinae nominationis. In
symbolica[54] theologia, quae sunt a sensibilibus in divina transnomina-
tiones, quae divinae formae, quae divinae figurae, et partes, et organa,
qui divini loci et mundi, qui furores, quae tristitiae et maniae, quae
ebrietates et crapulae, quae iuramenta, quae execrationes, qui somni,
quae vigiliae, et quaecunque aliae symbolicae sunt divinae similitudinis
sacre figuratae formationes. Et te arbitror considerasse, quomodo verbis
copiosiora magis sunt novissima primis. Etenim oportuit[55] theologicos
characteres, et divinorum nominum reserationem breviorem verbis esse
symbolica theologia. Quoniam quidem quantum ad superiora
respicimus, tantum verba contemplationibus[56] invisibilium coartantur:
Eloquiis — id est scripturis. Characteres — id est informationes. Divinis
nominibus — quid continet sermo de divinis nominibus. Symbolica theologia —
quid continet symbolica theologia. Organa — id est instrumenta. Mundi — id est
ornamenta. Maniae — id est insaniae. Execrationes — maledicta. Alia symbolice
— quare theologiae ac similitudines sive informationes. Novissima — Symbolicae
videlicet theologiae. Coartantur — id est deficiunt.

————. Quare theologici characteres sive informationes et sermo de divinis
nominibus paucorum versuum sint magis quam symbolica theologia.
Contemplationibus. Contemplationes sive conspectus intelligibilium theorias
quae immaterialem eorum simplicitatem decenter vocavit. Coartantur autem sive
desinunt pro subtrahuntur posuit.

sicut et nunc in ipsam super intellectum occidentes caliginem, non
brevem sermonem, sed sermonis defectum et nominationis inveniemus.
Nunc — id est in praesenti opere. Nominationis — sive intellectus.

————. Sermonis defectum ait non posse sermone quae sunt super sermonem com-
mendare. Porro nominationis defectum vel potius intellectus defectum dixit id quod
non valet intelligi — id est quod non potest aliquis intelligere, utpote super intellectum.

---

[54] symbolica] vero *add. A*
[55] oportuit] habere *D*
[56] contemplationibus] contemplationis *C*

characters. Then, in my work *On the Divine Names*: that it is named "ideal," that it is named ὤν,[37] that it is named "life," "wisdom," "power," and anything else that pertains to intelligible divine naming. In the *Symbolic Theology*: what the names are that cross from the sensuous to the divine; what the divine forms are; what the divine shapes, parts, and organs are; what the divine places and worlds are; what the rages are; what the griefs and ravings are; what the drinking bouts and hangovers are; what the oaths are; what the curses are; what the sleeps are; what the vigils are; and any other symbolic formations that sacredly shape the divine likeness. I think you have realized that the last of all are richer in words, more than the first. In fact, the *Theological Characters* and the untangling of the *Divine Names* had to be fewer in words than the *Symbolic Theology*, since, as we look up to higher and unseen things, our words are compressed by the contemplation of them.

Discourses — that is, the scriptures. Characters — that is, formations. *Divine Names* — what his work *On the Divine Names* contains. *Symbolic Theology* — what the *Symbolic Theology* contains. Organs — that is, instruments. Worlds — that is, orderings. Ravings — that is, insanities. Curses — maledictions. Other symbolic — why the theologies and likenesses or formations.[38] Last of all — the *Symbolic Theology*, you see. Are compressed — that is, they fail. *PG 4: 425.3*

———. Why the *Theological Characters* or *Formations* and the work *On the Divine Names* are of fewer lines than the *Symbolic Theology*. *PG 4: 425.4*

Contemplation. He has called "contemplation" or "inspection" of intelligibles the contemplation which befits immaterial simplicity. Now he has put "compressed" or "giving up" for "withheld." *PG 4: 425.6*

And now, as we fall into the very darkness above thought, we find not little speech, but a failure of speech and naming.[39]

Now — that is, in the present work. Naming — or thought.

———. He calls "failure of speech" the inability to mention in speech what is over speech. Further, he has called "failure of naming," or rather "of thought," what we are not able to think — that is, what no one can think, in that it is over thought. *PG 4: 425.7*

Et ibi quidem desursum ad novissima descendens sermo, iuxta quantitatem eius, quae est universaliter ad proportionalem multitudinem, inventus est. Nunc autem ab his, quae deorsum sunt, ad superpositum ascendens, secundum mensuram invii corripitur, et post omne invium totus sine voce erit, et totus adunabitur sono carenti. Quare autem omnino, inquis, ex praestantissimo ponentes[57] positiones, a novissimis inchoamus divinam ablationem?

Ibi — in theologico charactere sive doctrina vel informatione. Quantitatem — alia licta descensus. Invii — sive ascensionis. Invium — sive ascensionem. Positiones — id est affirmationes. Ablationem — id est negationem.

Ex praestantissimo. Praestantissimum sive primum ait id quod magis est proprium et ipsam cogitationem excedens, ut puta quia on est deus — id est est — quod et ipse se nominavit.

Positiones. Quomodo oporteat uti positionibus et ablationibus in deo. Et quia positiones quidem a praestantissimo sive optimo et quod magis cognatum est deo facimus, ablationes vero a[58] novissimis et magis ab eo distantibus.

Quia quid super omnem ponentes positionem, ex magis ipsi cognatiori conditionalem affirmationem oportuit ponere:

Quid — id est illud quod est.

Conditionalem. Quod Graecus hypotheticam habet et interpres conditionalem edidit quod magis exhortativam seu inductivam et suppositivam signat, et hic pro dictatoria et indicatoria positum est.

Affirmationem. Affirmatio Graece kataphasis dicitur.[59] Est autem kataphasis sermo pronunciatorius seu manifestatorius aut ex toto, aut repugnante, aut concinnante quoquam, aut conferente, ut puta Deus vita est, Deus bonitas est. Hypotheticus est sermo pronunciatorius[60] — id est universaliter — sive litigante aliquo, sive conhibente manifestatorius. Ergo hypothetica kataphasis in Deo est, quia Deus vita est et bonitas potius quam aer et lapis. Ablationes vero sive privationes per negationem dicuntur contra situm. Siquidem positiones sive situs, secundum causam, ut dictum est, per affirmationem dicuntur, quia vita deus

---

[57] ponentes] divinas *add. A*
[58] a] *om. D*
[59] dicitur] dicit *C*
[60] pronunciatorius] nunciatorius *D*

And here, as speech descends from above to the last of all, it is found in a mass proportionate to the quantity of the entirety of being.[40] Though now, as it ascends from below to what is set over it, the meter of the pathless grips it. After all the pathless, it will be wholly without a voice, and wholly united to the one who lacks sound. Why, you ask, do we begin the divine clearing off from the last of all, when we set down the settings starting from the most outstanding?

Here — in a theological character or doctrine or formation. Quantity — the other texts have "descent." Pathless — or "ascent." Pathless — or "ascent." Clearing off — that is, denial. Settings — that is, affirmations. *PG* 4: 425.8 (9–10)

From the most outstanding. He calls "most outstanding" or "first" that which is more proper and which exceeds knowledge itself.[41] For example, that God is ὤν — that is, "is" — which God even named himself. *PG* 4: 425.9

Settings. How we ought to use settings and clearings in God. Note also that we make settings from the most outstanding or ideal and what is most akin to God. But we make clearings from the last of all and most different from him. *PG* 4: 425.10

Because, when we set down something over all setting down, we had to set down a conditional affirmation arising from something more akin to it,

Something — that is, what is.

Conditional. Where the Greek has "hypothetical" and the translator gives "conditional," it marks what is more persuasive or compelling and suppositional. Here it is put for "spoken" and "signifying." Anast.

Affirmation. "Affirmation" is *kataphasis* in Greek. Now *kataphasis* is a declarative or revelatory speech, either itself a whole, or a rebuttal, or agreeing with something, or contributing to it. For example: "God is life;" "God is goodness." A hypothetical speech is a declarative speech, which reveals either without qualification, or by arguing against something, or by pulling it together. It is, then, a hypothetical *kataphasis* in God that God is "life" and "goodness" rather than "air" and "stone." Now the clearings or privations are said through denial, in opposition to the thesis. The settings or theses, of course, are said through affirmation, as I have said, pointing to a cause — that God is "life" rather than "air." In the settings, we begin in a more akin or adjacent manner: "life" and *PG* 4: 425.11 (1–25)

potius quam aer. Porro negativa privatio est, ut puta non inebriatur deus, non irascitur deus. Et in positionibus quidem magis cognate sive propinquius inchoamus. Familiarius sive magis proprium deo est vita et bonitas quam aer et lapis. In privationibus vero a novissimis et distantibus magis a deo remittimus, utpote[61] non sermone indicari deum, et non intelligi magis proprium deo est non crapulari, non irasci. Et tamen ex secundo privationis[62] incipimus, ut puta non inebriatur magis deus quam non dicitur, et non irascitur potius dicitur quam non intelligitur. Crapula ergo est multa et vehemens ebrietas, ut puta caput multum quoddam existens, quod est caput agitans et valde movens. Furia vero est non qualiscumque ira, sed pertinax.

> quod autem super omnem ablationem auferentes, ex magis ipso distantibus auferre. An non magis est vita et bonitas, quam aer et lapis? Et non magis non crapulae, et non maniae, quam non dicitur neque intelligitur?
>
> Quod — id est id quod est. Auferre — supple oportuit. Magis — ecce kataphasis et affirmatio seu positio.

Quam aer. Aer quidem est, secundum quod in regum libro dictum est: in aura levi sive tenui. Lapidem autem psalmista dixit. His ergo magis proprie positiones et manifestationes sunt in deo vita et bonitas. Sicut est in privatione ex contrario, utpote[63] crapulari et irasci, procul a deo et aliena. Non dici autem nec intelligi magis decens et proprium est deo, pro eo quod super omnem sensum sit et rationem.
Et magis non crapulae. Ecce depulsio sive negatio seu ablatio — id est privatio.

---

[61] utpote] *gr.* οἶον
[62] privationis] privationes *D*
[63] utpote] ut puta *A*

"goodness" are more familiar or proper to God than "air" and "stone." Now in the privations we return from the last of all and more distant from God, in that "God is not signified in speech," and "not understood," is more proper to God than "not to get hungover," "not to get angry." We begin, nevertheless, from the secondary privation: for example, God is called more "not drunk" than "not spoken." He is called "not angered" rather than "not understood." A "hangover," then, is a great and forceful drunkenness, as though it were a kind of multiple head, which is a shaking and actual moving of the head. Now "rage" is not anger of any sort, but stubborn anger.

> but when we cleared off something over all clearing off, to clear off from what differs more from it. Or is it not more "life" and "goodness" than "air" and "stone"? Is it not more "not hangovers" and "not ravings" than "it is neither spoken nor understood?"

Something — that is, what is. To clear off — add: "we had to." More — observe the *kataphasis* and affirmation or setting down.

Than "air." He is air, according to what the book of Kings says: *on a* light or *slender breeze.*[42] The psalmist calls him "stone."[43] "Life" and "goodness" are then more properly settings and revelations in God than these. Likewise, the contrary holds for privation, in that "to get hungover" and "angry" are far off from God and foreign. Now "not to be spoken" and "not to be understood" are more fitting and proper for God, in that he is over all sense and reason.   PG 4: 428.1

Is it not more "not hangovers." Observe the rejection, or denial, or clearing off — that is, privation.   ?

Capitulum IV

Quia nihil sensibilium omnis sensibilis
per excellentiam causalis

Chapter IV

*That what causes everything sensuous is,
through its excellence, not something sensuous*

Dicamus igitur sic: Omnium causa, et super omnia ens, neque carens essentia est, neque carens vita,

Causa — id est divinitas. Ens — id est existens.

Neque carens essentia. Necessario pater per haec praemunivit auditorem, ne caeteris depulsionibus opinaretur omnino non esse divinitatem, sed in his quidem esse ipsum supposuit, in illis autem illud quod nihil existentium sit, sed superessentialis.

neque irrationabilis est, neque insensualis, neque corpus est, neque figura, neque species, neque qualitatem, aut quantitatem, aut tumorem habet,[64]

Neque qualitas aut quantitas. Non est quantitas[65] quia plus quam quantitas est. Omnis enim quantitas tribus spatiis extenditur: longitudine quidem, latitudine, altitudine, quae iterum tria spatia senario protenduntur numero. Nam longitudo sursum et deorsum, latitudo dextrorsum et sinistrorsum, altitudo ante et retro protenditur. Deus autem omni spatio caret. Caret igitur quantitate. Item quantitas in numero partium aut naturaliter coniunctarum, ut est linea aut[66] tempus, aut naturaliter disiunctarum, ut sunt numeri, seu corporales seu intelligibiles.[67] Divina substantia nec continuis partibus componitur, nec dividuis distinguitur. Non est igitur quantitas. Quantitas tamen non incongrue denominatur duobus modis, aut quia quantitas saepe pro magnitudine virtutis ponitur, aut quia totius quantitatis principium est et causa. De qualitate quoque non aliter intelligendum. Nulla enim deus qualitas est, nulla ei accidit,[68] nullius est particeps. At vero saepissime qualitas de eo praedicatur, aut quia totius qualitatis conditor est, aut quod qualitas frequentissime in significatione virtutum ponitur, nam et bonitas et iustitia caeteraeque virtutes qualitates esse dicuntur. Deus autem virtus est et plus quam virtus.

Item. Quid itaque? Si quis de deo interrogaverit quantus vel qualis sit, num tibi recte videbitur responderi tantus et talis? Non illam dico quantitatem et qualitatem de qua propheta dicit: *magnus dominus et laudabilis nimis et magnitudinis*

---

64 tumorem habet] *om. C*
65 quantitas] omnium causa *add. D*
66 aut] et *D*
67 intelligibiles] constat *add. D*
68 accidit] et *add. D*

Let us say this, then: the cause of all things, and what is over all things, is neither "lacking being" nor "lacking life."

Cause — that is, the divinity. What is — that is, the real.

Neither "lacking being." Father Dionysius had to forewarn his hearer through this, so that he might not guess from the rest of the rejections that there is no divinity at all. In these he sets down being itself, while in the others he sets down what is not a reality but over being. *PG 4: 428.2*

It is neither unreasoning nor senseless. It is neither body, nor shape, nor definition. It has neither quality, quantity, nor bulk.

Neither quality, quantity. It is not quantity because it is more than quantity. For every quantity is extended in three dimensions: height, breadth, and depth. These three dimensions are extended again to the number of six. For height is extended up and down, breadth is extended right and left, and depth is extended forward and backward. Now God lacks all dimension, and so he lacks quantity. Quantity, moreover, lies in a number of parts either naturally joined together, as a line or time is, or naturally disjoined, as bodily or intelligible numbers are. The divine substance is neither compounded of continuous parts nor sliced up by divided parts, and so it is not quantity. It is, nevertheless, not unsuitably named "quantity" for two reasons: either because quantity is often put for greatness of virtue, or because it is the principle and cause of all quantity. About quality, too, we should think nothing else, for God is not a quality. None befalls him; he participates in none. But we also very often predicate quality of him, either because he is the founder of all quality or because quality is very regularly put into the meaning of the virtues. For goodness, justice, and the other virtues are said to be qualities. Now God is virtue and more than virtue. *PP I.86.31–88.13*

On the same topic. What, then? If someone should ask of God, how much or of what sort he is, surely it would not seem right to you that we respond: "this much" and "of such a sort"? I do not mean the quantity and quality about which the prophet says: *the Lord is great and ever so praiseworthy, and there is no limit to* *PP II.146.24–148.11*

eius non est finis. Vide quam alte theologus loquitur. *Magnus* inquit *dominus,* sed ne quis finita quantitate eum finiri putaret, continuo addidit:[69] *et magnitudinis eius non est finis.* Item ne quis qualitatem finitam in eo esse opinaretur, non dixit simpliciter *et laudabilis* sed adiunxit *nimis.* Nimis autem dicitur quod omnem modum excedit. Non illam itaque ut dixi quantitatem infinitam nomino nec illam qualitatem quae est nimis, sed qualitatem et quantitatem quae secundum accidens[70] in subiecto dicuntur. Non quidem recte sic respondetur. Ubi enim non invenitur diffinita substantia vel, ut ita dicam, diffinitum subiectum, ibi quantitatem et qualitatem quaerere et firmare stultum valde risuque dignum mihi videtur, ac per hoc dum in deo nullus intellectus diffinitam substantiam vel, ut ita dicam, diffinitum subiectum secundum quod dici vel intelligi valeat quid sit reperire non potest, nonne limpidissime claret nullam finitam vel infinitam quantitatem, nullam qualitatem finitam vel infinitam in ipso cognosci ab aliquo valere? Si enim omnem finitam vel infinitam substantiam infinita et plus quam infinita propriae virtutis excellentia superexaltat, quis non continuo ac sine dubitatione erumpat ut aperte fateatur atque exclamet nullam finitam vel infinitam quantitatem vel qualitatem in eum cadere?

neque in loco est,[71] neque videtur,

Neque in loco. Omni loco caret divina natura, quamvis intra se ipsam omnia quae ab ea sunt collocet, ideoque omnium locus dicitur. Se ipsam tamen non nescit locare, quia infinita est et incircumscripta et in nullo intellectu locari se — id est diffiniri et circumscribi — permittit. Ab ipsa siquidem infinita et plus quam infinita omnia finita et infinita procedunt, inque ipsam infinitam et plus quam infinitam redeunt.

neque tactum sensibilem habet, neque sentitur, neque sensibilis est, neque inordinationem habet, neque perturbationem a passionibus materialibus commota, neque impotens est sensibilibus succumbens casibus, neque indigens est lucis, neque mutationem, aut corruptionem, aut partitionem, aut privationem, aut fluxum, neque aliud quid sensibilium est, neque habet.

---

[69] addidit] addit *D*
[70] accidens] est *add. D*
[71] est] *om. C*

his greatness.[44] See how profoundly the theologian speaks! *The Lord is great*, he says, and so that no one may suppose that he is limited by a finite quantity, he adds at once: *and there is no limit to his greatness.* Moreover, so that no one may guess that there is a finite quality in him, he does not simply say: *and praiseworthy*, but he joins to it: *ever so.* Now God is called "ever so" because he surpasses all qualification. As I have said, then, I do not mean that infinite quantity or that quality which is "ever so." I mean the quality and quantity which are said of accidents in a subject. No one would rightly give such a response. For where we find no defined substance or, so to speak, defined subject, it seems quite foolish to me and worthy of laughter to seek to affirm quantity and quality here. For this reason, since no intellect is able to find a defined substance or, so to speak, a defined subject in God so that it could say or think what he is, are we not clearly enlightened that no one can know in it any finite or infinite quantity, any finite or infinite quality? For if the infinite and more than infinite rises by the excellence of its own virtue over every finite or infinite substance, who would not burst out at once and without hesitation, that he may openly confess and exclaim that no finite or infinite quantity or quality applies to it?

It is neither in a place, nor is it seen.

Neither in a place. The divine nature lacks all place, although it roots within it everything that arises from it, and so it is called the place of all things. Though it is infinite and uncircumscribed, it is nevertheless not ignorant of how to place itself. It allows itself to be placed — that is, defined and circumscribed — in no intellect. You see, from the infinite itself and the more than infinite all finite and infinite things proceed, and they return to the infinite itself and the more than infinite. *PP* II.150.23–8

> It neither has a sense of touch, nor is it sensed, nor is it sensuous. It has neither the disorder nor the trouble of what is moved by material passions. It is not powerless, like what yields to sensible events. It needs no light. It is not and has not: change, decay, partition, privation, flux, or whatever else belongs to sensuous things.

Capitulum V

Quia nihil intelligibilium omnis intelligibilis
per excellentiam causalis

Chapter V

*That what causes everything intelligible is,
through its excellence, not something intelligible*

Iterum autem ascendentes dicamus ὠν neque anima est, neque intellectus,

On — id est existens scilicet divinitas.

————. Omnes has incorporales privationes oportet non humiliter intelligere, sed in singulis quae dicta sunt subaudire, quod ipse pater ait. Et Graecus habet: neque aliud quid eorum quae nobis insunt aut alicui existentium est cognitum. Omnia enim quae dicta sunt ex deo sunt. Et quomodo ipsum[72] ex ipso[73] erit?

neque phantasiam, aut opinionem, aut verbum, aut intelligentiam habet, neque ratio est, neque intelligentia, neque dicitur, neque intelligitur,

————. Phantasiarum duae sunt species, quarum nulla cadit in deum earum. Prima est quae ex sensibili natura[74] primo in instrumentis sensuum nascitur et imago in sensibus expressa proprie vocatur. Altera vero est ipsa quae consequenti ordine ex praedicta imagine formatur et est ipsa phantasia quae proprie sensus interior consuevit nominari. Et illa prior corpori semper adhaeret, posterior vero animae. Et prior quamvis in sensu sit se ipsam non sentit. Posterior vero et se ipsam sentit et priorem suscipit.

neque numerus est, neque ordo, neque magnitudo, neque parvitas, neque aequalitas, neque[75] similitudo aut dissimilitudo, neque stat, neque movetur, neque silentium ducit, neque habet virtutem, neque virtus est,

————. Deus enim numerum in se non recipit, quoniam solus innumerabilis est, et numerus sine numero, et supra omnem numerum causa omnium numerorum.

————. Divina siquidem natura sibi ipsi sufficit ad habendum nec ulla virtus ei accidit, quoniam in se ipsa simplicissima virtus et plus quam virtus subsistit et fons omnium virtutum, et quaecumque substantia virtutem possidet non aliunde habet nisi ex participatione generalium virtutum, quas omnium causalis virtus in primordialibus suis condidit principiis.

---

[72] ipsum] *gr.* αὐτός
[73] ipso] *gr.* αὐτῶν
[74] natura] est *D*
[75] neque] sed *D*

Now, ascending again, let us say that ὤν[45] is neither soul nor intellect.

ὤν — that is, the real divinity, you understand.

————. We should not think of all these bodiless privations in a lowly way, but should surmise in each the things that have been said, as Father Dionysius himself says. The Greek has: "nor do we know any other of those that are in us or any realities."[46] For all the things he mentions arise from God. So how will this arise from that?[47]

PG 4: 425.11
(26–9, 31–3)

It has neither imagination, nor opinion, nor a word, nor intelligence. It is neither reason nor intelligence, neither spoken nor thought.

————. There are two kinds of imagination, neither of which applies to God. The first is what originates first in the sense organs from a sensuous object in nature, and it is properly called the image expressed in the senses. Now the other is what is formed next in order from the aforesaid image, and this is properly the imagination which is customarily named interior sense. The former always clings to the body, but the latter clings to the soul. Though the former is in the sense, it does not sense itself, but the latter both senses itself and supports the former.

PP II.108.8–15

It is neither number, nor rank, nor greatness, nor smallness, nor equality, nor likeness or unlikeness. It neither rests nor moves. It does not keep silent. It neither has virtue nor is virtue.

————. For God does not accept number into himself, since he alone is numberless. The cause of all numbers is a number without number and over every number.

PP I.208.12–4

————. The divine nature is, of course, sufficient in itself for possession of virtue. No virtue befalls it, since the simplest virtue and more than virtue subsists in it, and it is the font of all the virtues. Whatever substance possesses a virtue has it from nowhere else than participation in the general virtues, which the virtue that causes them all has founded in its primordial principles.

PP II.150.18–22

neque lux, neque vivit,[76] neque vita est, neque hostia est,

———. Divinitas Christi necnon et patris et spiritus sancti unius dei totius purgationis et illuminationis et perfectionis est principium, non quod illa hostia — id est divinitas — ulli superiori se immoletur, quia supra se nihil est, sed quia eo modo loquendi quo causa per effectum significatur hostia dicitur. Ac per hoc, quoniam ipsa causa et principium purgationis est, non incongrue purgatio dicitur et hostia, cum plusquam hostia sit. Hinc ipse Dionysius in negationibus mysticae theologiae ait neque hostia est, volens de ea praedicare plusquam hostiam esse et hostiarum principium.

neque saeculum, neque tempus,

———. Tempore caret ea natura quae se ignorat principium habere vel finem et omnem motum quo movetur omne quod a principio ad finem et in finem movetur. Nescit in se incrementa quae fiunt per numeros locorum et temporum vel detrimenta, quoniam in se ipsa plena atque perfecta est.

neque tactus est eius intelligibilis, neque scientia, neque veritas est, neque regnum, neque sapientia, neque unum, neque unitas, neque deitas, aut bonitas,

———. Negabis duo proloquia sibimet adversantia dum de deo praedicantur vera simul esse et ullo modo falsa, quamquam ambo eiusdem virtutis non sint, ut puta deus veritas est, deus veritas non est? Credo quia non negabis, dum ipse de seipso dicat: *ego sum via et veritas et vita.* Sanctus autem areopagita Dionysius in mystica theologia dicit quia deus neque veritas est neque vita. Ait enim: "neque virtus est, neque lux, neque vita," et paulo post: "neque scientia est, neque veritas." Numquid Dionysius contradicit Christo, qui de seipso praedicat seipsum veritatem esse? Absit. Utrumque enim verum est deus veritas est, deus veritas non est. Nec solum verum, sed etiam verissimum. Unum quidem dictum est secundum affirmationem per metaforam, quoniam ipse conditor est et causa primordialis veritatis, cuius participatione vera sunt quaecumque vera sunt omnia. Alterum autem per negationem quae est secundum excellentiam, quia plus est quam veritas. Ac per hoc et verum est deus veritas est, dum sit omnium

---

[76] neque vivit] *om.* D

It is neither light nor life, nor is it a victim.[48]

————. The divinity of Christ no less than the Father and the Holy Spirit — the one God — is the principle of all purification, illumination and perfection. The victim — that is, the divinity — is not offered to any superior, since nothing is over it. Rather, it is called "victim" by that mode of speaking by which the cause is signified through its effect. Since it is the very cause and principle of purification, it is not unsuitably called, through this mode, "purification" and "victim," although it is more than a victim. For this reason, Dionysius himself in the denials of the *Mystical Theology* says: "nor is it a victim," wishing to say of it that it is both more than a victim and the principle of victims.

Exp. III.58.74–83

It is neither age nor time.

————. That nature lacks time which does not know that it has a beginning, end, and every motion which moves everything that is moved from a beginning to an end and into an end. It does not understand in itself the gains and losses that come about in a series of places and times, since in itself it is full and perfect.

PP II.150.29–33

There is neither understanding nor an intelligible touch of it. It is neither truth, nor kingdom, nor wisdom, nor one, nor unity, nor deity or goodness.

————. Will you deny that claims opposed to one another are both true and in no way false when predicated of God, though they are not of the same power? As, for example: "God is truth," and "God is not truth"? I do not think you will deny it, since he says of himself: *I am the way, the truth, and the life.*[49] Now St. Dionysius the Areopagite in his *Mystical Theology* says that God is neither truth nor life. For he says: "he is neither virtue, nor light, nor life," and a little later: "he is neither understanding nor truth." Does Dionysius contradict Christ, who predicates of himself that he is truth? Far from it. For "God is truth" and "God is not truth" are both true, and not only true, but even supremely true. One has said through the metaphor of affirmation that he is the founder and primordial cause of truth, by participation in which every truth whatsoever is true. Now the other has said through the denial that is of excellence that he is more than truth. For this reason, both "God is truth" is true, since he is the cause of all true

PP IV.36.31–38.20

verorum causa, et verum est deus veritas non est, quia superat omne quod dicitur et intelligitur et est. Quod autem superius dictum est: "quamquam ambo non eiusdem virtutis sint," sic accipe. Minus enim valet ad ineffabilis divinae essentiae significationem affirmatio quam[77] negatio, quoniam una ex creaturis ad creatorem transfertur, altera ultra omnem creaturam de creatore per seipsum praedicatur.

Item. Deus veritas dicitur, non tamen proprie. Veritati etenim[78] falsitas opponitur et per hoc proprie veritas non est. ὑπεραληθες igitur est et ὑπεραληθεια, hoc est plus quam verus et plus quam veritas. Eadem ratio de omnibus divinis nominibus observanda est.

———. De sapientia quoque nulla alia occurrit ratio, ideoque de deo proprie praedicari non est arbitrandum, quoniam sapientiae et sapienti insipiens et insipientia oppugnant. Proinde ypersophos — id est plusquam sapiens — et ypersophia — id est plusquam sapientia — recte vereque dicitur.

———. Distant ab invicem unum et unitas. Alterum siquidem indicat subiectum, alterum vero talem qualitatem, sicut album et albedo, bonum et bonitas.

———. Notandum quod nec deitas essentia est dei, quemadmodum nec bonitas nec aliud quid ex his quae dicta sunt. Aliter notandum quia neque deitas substantia est, veluti nec unum quid eorum quae dicta sunt, nec ex his quae illis adversantia sunt, propter quod nullum eorum est. Non enim est essentia eius, sed gloria sive opinio de eo, ut etiam Sextus ecclesiasticus philosophus ait.

———. Bonitas deus dicitur sed proprie bonitas non est. Bonitati enim malitia opponitur. ὑπεραγαθος igitur est — id est plusquam bonus — et ὑπεραγαθοτητα — id est plusquam bonitas.

> neque spiritus est, sicut nos scimus, neque filiolitas, neque paternitas, neque aliud quid nobis aut alicui existentium cognitum,

———. Licet enim ipse dixerit spiritus est deus, et sanctus spiritus sic vocetur, sed non est nobis per essentiam notus, sed nec supernis virtutibus.

———. Notandum quod neque spiritus neque filietas neque paternitas sit, sicut non scimus sive sicuti nos agnoscenda.

———. Sicut nos scimus in omni sententia eorum quae proposita sunt accipe. Designat autem quod ait sicut nos scimus sive sicuti nos intelligenda, ac si diceret secundum nostram scientiam.

---

[77] quam] quamquam *D*
[78] etenim] enim *D*

things, and "God is not truth" is true, because he overcomes all that is said and thought and is. Now as to what I said above: "although both are not of the same power" — take it this way. For affirmation is less able than denial to signify the indescribable divine being, since one is ferried from creatures to the creator, while the other is predicated of the creator in himself, beyond every creature.

————. God is called "truth," but not properly, for falsehood is opposed to *PP* I.78.10–3
truth, and for this reason properly he is not truth. He is then ὑπεραλήθης and ὑπεραλήθεια — that is, more than true and more than truth. We ought to maintain the same structure for all the divine names.

————. For wisdom, too, there is no other structure, and so we ought to judge *PP* I.78.16–20
that it is not properly predicated of God, since "foolish" and "foolishness" counteract "wisdom" and "wise." For this reason, he is rightly and truly said to be ὑπέρσοφος — that is, "more than wise" — and ὑπερσοφία — that is, "more than wisdom."

————. "One" and "unity" differ from each other. The one, of course, indicates *PG* 4: 429.1 (1–4)
a subject, but the other indicates a certain quality, like "white" and "whiteness," "good" and "goodness."

————. Note that "deity" is not the being of God, just as "goodness" is not, or *PG* 4: 429.1 (4–9)
any other of the things he has said. Again, note that the deity is not "substance," just as it is not one of the things that have been said or one of the things opposed to them, and so it is none of them. For substance is not his being, but a glory or guess about him, as even Sextus the Ecclesiastical Philosopher says.

————. God is said to be "goodness," but properly he is not goodness. For *PP* I.76.33–5
"wickedness" is opposed to "goodness." He is then ὑπεράγαθος — that is, "more than good" — and ὑπεραγαθότητα — that is, "more than goodness."

It is neither spirit — as we understand it — nor sonship, nor fatherhood, nor anything else that we or any reality may know.

————. For although the Spirit is itself God, and so is called the "Holy Spirit," *PG* 4: 429.3 (49–52)
we and the lofty powers still do not know it in its being.

————. Note that it is neither "spirit" nor "sonship" nor "fatherhood," either as *PG* 4: 429.2 (1–3)
we do not understand them, or as we know them.

————. Take "as we understand it" of everything he has proposed. This is the *PG* 4: 429.2 (3–5)
meaning of what he says: "as we understand it" or "as must be thought," as though he were to say: "following our understanding."

neque quid non existentium,[79] neque quid existentium est,[80] neque existentia eam cognoscunt, an ipsa est,[81] neque ipsa cognoscit existentia, an existentia sunt,[82]

Eam — id est causa omnium. An ipsa est — id est sicut ipsa est. An existentia sit — id est ex eo quod ipsa sunt sed ex se ipsa superessentialiter.

————. Neque existentia eam cognoscunt aut ipsa est sive quam ipsa sit,[83] nec ipsa cognoscit existentia an existentia sint. Neque enim cognoscunt trinitatem an ipsa sit — id est nihil est ut ipsa ut cognoscant eam an ipsa sit. Nos enim cognoscimus quidem quid sit humanitas, siquidem humanitas sumus. Existentia[84] vero trinitatis nescimus[85] quid sit. Non enim sumus essentiae ipsius. Ita neque deus novit existentia an sint. Non enim est quid existentium non[86] secundum ipsa.

————. Quoniam dixit neque existentia cognoscunt causam sive auctorem omnium. Hoc perdictio est evidens — id est non cognoscere deum. Breviter curavit quod ineptum vel dissimile videbatur, dicens an ipsa[87] sit — id est nullus existentium cognoscit deum, sicuti est, hoc est incognoscibilem et superessentialem[88] essentiam eius, sive existentiam secundum quam existit. Hoc enim est quod ait dominus: *et nemo novit filium nisi pater, neque patrem quis novit, nisi filius*. Deinceps e contrario infert magnus Dionysius, et ait quod nemo noscat deum ex his quae sunt secundum quod est, sic nec ipse deus novit existentia an existentia sint — id est nescit conferens productis a se essentiis ipsas essentias quid sint — sed supermundane ac super intellectum. Denique nos scimus existentia sensibiliter per tactum et per reliquos sensus conferentes quantitatibus et qualitatibus et contrarietatibus seu similitudinibus et furiis et humoribus et caeteris. Angeli vero scienter et immaterialiter ea sciunt, non sicut nos sensibiliter. Ita ergo et deus incomparabiliter et superexcellenter, non tamen essentiis conferendo novit existentia.

---

[79] existentium] est *omisi ex E*
[80] est] *om. D*
[81] an ipsa est] aut existentia sit *D*
[82] sunt] sint *D*
[83] sit] nec ipsa sit *add. C*
[84] existentiam] *gr.* ὕπαρξιν
[85] nescimus] nec scimus *A*
[86] non] *gr.* ἤ
[87] ipsa] ipse *A*
[88] superessentialem] supersubstantialem *A*

It is neither an unreality nor a reality. Realities do not know it as it is, and it does not know realities as realities are.

It — that is, the cause of all things. As it is — just as it is. As realities are — that is, from the fact that they are, but from itself, in a manner over being.

————. Realities do not know it as it is or how it is, and it does not know realities as realities are. For they do not know the trinity as it is — that is, there is nothing like it, so that they may know it as it is. For we know what humanity is, since we are human. But we do not understand what the reality of the trinity is, for we are not of its being. Neither, then, does God know realities as they are, for he is neither a reality nor like them. *PG* 4: 429.3 (41–9)

————. Since he has said that realities do not know the cause or author of all things. This — that is, not to know God — is visibly our ruin. He quickly redeems this apparent gaffe or unlikeness by saying "as it is" — that is, no reality knows God as he is, meaning his unknowable being over being, or the reality in which he exists. For this is what the Lord says: *no one knows the Son except the Father, nor does anyone know the Father, except the Son.*[50] Then, the great Dionysius brings in the contrary, and says that no one, starting from the things that are, knows God in what he is, so neither does God himself know realities as realities are. That is, as he assembles his productions, he does not understand what the beings themselves are by starting from the beings. He knows them over the intellect in a manner over this world. Finally, we understand realities sensuously. Through touch and the remaining senses, we assemble quantities or qualities, and opposites or likenesses, and rages, humors, and the rest. But the angels understand them with understanding and immaterially, not sensuously as we do. And so, God, then, knows realities incomparably and over excellence, but not by assembling their beings. *PG* 4: 429.3 (6–21, 28–32)

neque verbum eius est, neque nomen, neque scientia,

————. Quando interrogamus quid est hoc vel illud, nihil aliud videmur quaerere nisi aut iam diffinitam substantiam aut diffiniri valentem. Si ergo nemo sapientium generaliter de omni essentia inquirit quid sit, quoniam diffiniri non potest, sed ex circumstantiis suis intra quas veluti terminos circumscribitur, loco dico et tempore, quanto et quali, relatione, copulatione, statu, motu, habitu, caeterisque accidentibus quibus ipsa ratione subiecti substantia per seipsam incognita indiffinibilisque subsistens esse tantum, non autem quid sit, manifestatur, quis theologiae disciplinis eruditus interrogare praesumat de divina substantia quid sit, cum purissime intelligat de ipsa nec diffiniri posse nec ullum eorum quae sunt esse omniaque quae diffiniri possunt superare? Quiescat omnis anima ab omni ratione eorum quae circa deum sunt temere in diffinitionem eius insilire, sed silentio colat tantum ineffabilem et super intellectum omnisque summum scientiae divinae essentiae veritatem. Si ergo nemo sapientissimorum potest cognoscere existentium substantiae rationes secundum quas fundatae sunt, quis verbo deum audeat in aliquo diffinire?

————. Ascripta scilicet essentiae[89] deitatis.

————. Nemo pie cognoscentium inque divina mysteria introductorum, audiens de deo seipsum intelligere non posse quid sit, aliud debet existimare nisi ipsum deum qui non est quid omnino eorum quae sunt ignorare in seipso quod ipse non est. Seipsum autem non cognoscit aliquid esse. Nescit igitur quid ipse est, hoc est nescit se quid esse, quoniam cognoscit se nullum eorum quae in aliquo cognoscuntur et de quibus dici potest vel intelligi quid sunt omnino esse. Nam si in aliquo seipsum cognosceret, non omnino infinitum et incomprehensibilem innominabilemque seipsum indicaret. Ut: *quid interrogas* inquit *nomen meum*? Et: *hoc est mirabile*. Aut nonne hoc vere est mirabile nomen quod est super omne nomen, quod innominabile, quod omni supercollocatum nomini nominato sive in saeculo hoc sive in futuro? Si ergo increpat quaerere nomen suum quia super omne nomen est innominabile, quid si quis quaerat eius substantiam, quae si in aliquo finito esset, finito nomine non careret? Quoniam vero in nullo substituuntur, quia infinitus omni nominatione caret, quia innominabilis est. Omne siquidem quod in aliquo substantialiter intelligitur ita ut proprie de eo praedicetur quid sit, neque modum neque mensuram excedit. Aliquo namque modo quo finitur concluditur, aliqua mensura quam superare non potest lineatur.

---

[89] essentiae] essentia *A*

There is neither a word for it, nor a name, nor understanding.

————. When we ask "what is this?" or "what is that?" we seem to seek nothing but a defined substance or one able to be defined. If, then, no one wise asks of every being "what is it?" in general, since it cannot be defined, but is encompassed, within certain limits, as it were, by its circumstances — I mean place and time, quantity and quality, relation, junction, rest, motion, disposition, and the rest of the accidents by which a substance, unknowable in itself and subsisting without definition in the structure of its subject, is revealed as to its being alone, not as to what it is — what scholar of the discipline of theology would presume to ask "what is it?" of the divine substance, since he thinks of it in purity, that it cannot be defined, it is not one of the things that are, and it overcomes everything that can be defined? Each soul must cease to jump rashly to a definition of God from the structure of all that surrounds him, and, in silence, cultivate the truth of the divine being alone, a truth which is indescribable, over the intellect, and the highest understanding of all.[51] If, then, no one wise can know the structure of the substance of realities according to which they have been founded, who would dare to define God in any word?

————. The being of the deity is unwritten, you see.

————. No one who knows piously, and has been introduced to the divine mysteries, when he hears of God that he cannot think of what he is, ought to conclude anything other than that God himself, who is altogether none of the things that are, does not know in himself what he is not. Now he does not know that he is something. He does not understand, then, what he himself is — that is, he does not understand that he is a "what," since he knows that he is none of the things that are known in anything and about which we can say or think at all what they are. For if he were to know himself in something, it would indicate that he was not altogether infinite, ungraspable, and nameless. As when he says: *why do you ask my name?*[52] And: *it is marvelous.*[53] Or is that name not truly marvelous which is over every name, which is nameless, and which is rooted over every name that can be named whether in this age or in the age to come? If, then, he rebukes those who seek his name, since it is nameless over every name, what if someone should seek his substance, which would not lack a finite name if it were in something finite? But since he is established in nothing because he is infinite, he lacks all naming because he is nameless. Everything, you see, which is thought of something substantially, so that what it is may be predicated properly of it, surpasses neither mode nor measure. For it is closed in by some qualification which limits it. It is delineated by some measure which it cannot overcome.

PP II.136.24–138.13

?

PP II.142.35–144.16

neque tenebrae est, neque lumen, neque error, neque veritas,

————. Quomodo superius dicens non est lux et iterum non est veritas, descendens huc rursus ait non sunt[90] tenebrae, neque lux, neque error, neque veritas, huius solutionem habes in descriptione subsequenti.

Lux. Superius cum dixisset, non est lux, et iterum non est veritas, descendens huc iterum ait non est tenebrae, neque lux, neque error, neque veritas. Exquiro ergo nequid primum de absolute intellecto dicat, ut puta ut substantiae angelorum, et veritatem eandem incausative et absolute intellectam veritatem. Porro caetera, quia neque eorum quae ad aliquid sunt, ut puta ex tenebris[91] lucem, ac si[92] ex illa quae virtute in eam quae operatione est lux transferens ex affectualibus in alterna lucem ac tenebras. Non enim caligo est, neque luminis multitudo, sic nec ex contrario, ex eo qui virtute est error in eam quae ex operatione est veritas. Omnia enim haec secunda[93] sive posteriora eo sunt, ex ipso provide commeantia.

neque est eius universaliter positio, neque ablatio, sed eorum, quae post eam sunt, positiones et ablationes facientes, ipsam neque auferimus, neque ponimus, quoniam et super omnem positionem est perfecta et singularis omnium causa, et[94] super omnem ablationem excellentia omnium simpliciter perfectione, et summitas omnium.

Ipsam — essentiam eius.

---

[90] sunt] *gr.* ἔστι
[91] tenebris] transducens *add. A*
[92] ac si] aut *C*
[93] secunda] eius *add. A*
[94] et] *om. D*

It is neither shadows nor light, nor error, nor truth.

————. How did he earlier say "he is not light," and again, "he is not truth,"   *?*
but now, descending, he says again: "he is not shadows, nor light, nor error, nor
truth?" You have the unravelling of this in the description that follows.

————. Although he said earlier: "he is not light," and again, "he is not truth,"   *PG* 4: 429.3 (52–65)
now, descending, he says again: "he is not shadows, nor light, nor error, nor
truth." I wonder, then, if it can be that he speaks first about the free intellect[54]
— the substances of the angels, for example — and the same sort of truth, the
truth thought of causelessly and freely. Then, in the latter, that he is not something aimed at something — for example, drawing his light from the shadows,
as though he brings the light from its power to its activity, and makes light and
shadows cross from their partners into each other. For he is not darkness, nor a
multitude of lights, and so he does not arise from a contrary, crossing from what
is error in potency to what is truth in activity. For his foresight routes them all
from him, and they are second to him, or after him.

There is no setting down or clearing off of it at all. When we make
settings and clearings of what comes after it, we neither clear it off
nor set it down, since the perfect unique cause of all things is over
all setting down, and, simply put, the summit of all things and what
excels the perfection of all things is over all clearing off.
It — its being.

NOTES

[1] Matth. 11:27.

[2] *PG* 43: 137C–140A.

[3] The thirteenth-century edition omits the crucial *per*. The sentence should read: "we, like a kind of sacrifice, return to their unity through θέωσις — that is, deification."

[4] Eph. 4:13.

[5] Ps. 147:15.

[6] Eph. 2:8.

[7] Ps. 118:49.

[8] Rom. 5:5.

[9] Ps. 84:9.

[10] The extant codices omit *caliginem*. The sentence should read: "here he calls it the mistiest and unseen darkness."

[1] Ps. 96:2.

[12] Ps. 17:11.

[13] Perhaps the prayer of the anaphora in the Byzantine liturgy. For another explanation of "many-eyed," see *PG* 4: 188.4.

[14] *De Vera Religione*, 55.113 (*CCSL* 32, p. 259).

[15] Ioh. 12:26.

[16] "Of the mind" is Eriugena's addition.

[17] He refers to scholium 421.1 of the *Mystical Theology*. I find no reference to unknowing in the scholia to the fifth chapter of *On the Divine Names*.

[18] Eriugena reads οἰομένους ("they suppose") as οἷς μὲν οὕς ("as for them — those").

[19] Ps. 17:12.

[20] *PG* 4: 216.10; 244.7; 340.5; 341.1; 361.2. See Appendix B.

[21] *CH* 13, 1–2 (141A) and its scholia: *PG* 4: 40.12; 41.1. See Appendix B.

[122] The thirteenth-century edition reads *manifestat* as *manifestet*. The sentence should read: "he brings in a witness, as the 'says' reveals."

[23] Anastasius translates ἔφη ("said") as φησί ("says"), which renders the statement meaningless. The scholium means to say that Dionysius would refer to Bartholomew's spoken words in the past tense, but to his written words in the present tense.

[24] This assertion, found only in the thirteenth-century edition, undoes the tidy distinction which precedes it. In the Greek original and the earlier tradition of the Anastasian scholia the whole section reads: "likewise, if πρωτότοκος — that is, *prototokos* — has its accent on the antepenult, it means 'firstborn.' But if the accent of πρωτοτόκος is put on the penult, it suggests a woman who gave birth to her firstborn, as Homer, too, demonstrates: πρωτοτόκος κινύρη οὐ πρὶν εἰδυῖα τόκοιο."

[25] Eriugena reads αὐτῷ μὲν οὐ συγγίνεται ("he does not come to be") as οὕτω μένουσι γίνεται ("while they remain, he comes to be").

[26] *PG* 4: 33.10. See Appendix B.

[27] Eriugena reads τότε ("then") as ὅτι ("that").

[28] Eriugena reads ἀπομύει as though it came from ἀπομυέω ("teach") and not ἀπόμνυμι ("abandon").

²⁹ *PG* 4: 216.10; 352.2; 352.3; 245.3; 264.1; 340.5; 224.6. See Appendix B.

³⁰ Eriugena reads ἑνούμενος ("united") as νούμενου ("than intellection"). The Greek reads: "united for the better to what is altogether unknown to all understanding in idleness."

³¹ Eriugena reads γινώσκων ("knowing") as γινωσκόντων ("of those who know"). The Greek reads: "knowing over the soul by knowing nothing."

³² Eriugena reads θέαν ("vision") as θεόν ("God").

³³ Anastasius simply transliterates the Greek τίμια, meaning "precious."

³⁴ Eriugena reads γνωστῶν ("knowing") as ἀγνωστῶν ("unknowing").

³⁵ Ps. 44:2.

³⁶ Ioh. 15:26.

³⁷ "Being."

³⁸ This seemingly incomplete comment is really a garbled version of the first few words in the scholium below it (*PG* 4: 425.4).

³⁹ Eriugena reads ἀνοησίαν ("failure of intellection") as ἀὀνόμασιαν ("failure of naming").

⁴⁰ Eriugena reads καθόδου ("way down") as καθόλου ("entirety").

⁴¹ Anastasius translates προεισβάλλοντος as "exceeds" rather than "first enters." The idea that the first aspect of an object to enter the mind is its being appears elsewhere in the scholia: cf. 317.1 (9–10); 401.3 (10–3).

⁴² III Reg. 19:12.

⁴³ Ps. 118:22.

⁴⁴ Ps. 144:3.

⁴⁵ "Being."

⁴⁶ This statement is Anastasius' summary of a longer passage in Greek which he has omitted.

⁴⁷ The extant codices garble the question, substituting *ipsum* and *ipso* for *ipse* and *ipsis*. The question should read: "so how will God arise from them?"

⁴⁸ Eriugena reads the Greek οὐσία ("being") as ὅστια ("victim").

⁴⁹ Ioh. 14:6.

⁵⁰ Matth. 11:27.

⁵¹ This is an unacknowledged quotation from Maximus the Confessor's *Liber Ambiguorum*: *PG* 91: 1225D1–1228A3.

⁵² Gen. 32:29.

⁵³ Iud. 13:18.

⁵⁴ Migne's text has φῶς ("light") here, not νοῦς ("intellect").

Appendix A: Omitted Scholia

Source Unknown
On: "shadows"[1]
Read the preceding scholium at the letter "T."[2]

Source Unknown
On: "their contrived treacheries"[3]
Read the preceding scholium at such a mark.[4]

Source Unknown
On: "much and the least"[5]
How it is "much and the least."

PG 4: 420.6 (1–3)
On: "the divine Moses"[6]
Note how he recounts the story of Moses: that Moses knew God, so far as a human may, when he went up onto the mountain and went into the darkness.

PG 4: 425.2
On: "Jesus, who is over being"[7]
Note that he writes against the Nestorians and Acephali.

PG 4: 425.5
On: "than the *Symbolic Theology*"[8]
He means the first things in the *Symbolic Theology*.

---

[1] See above, p. 59.
[2] The Parisian manuscripts do not preserve any scholium marked with the letter "T," but the relevant scholium is surely *PG* 4: 416.7 (9–11).
[3] See above, p. 61.
[4] The preceding scholium is *PG* 4: 420.1 (1–4).
[5] See above, p. 63.
[6] See above, p. 67.
[7] See above, p. 85.
[8] See above, p. 87.

PG 4: 425.8 (1–9)
On: "and here, as speech descends from above"[9]

Because the intelligibles are also henads of the God over intellect, and God is one, or even over unity. He is, of course, compressed, seeing that he is both partless and undivided. But to the degree that things beneath God descend into the sensuous, they dwell rather in the partitioned and scattered. They are multiplied by multiplicities that lead them into the partition and branching out of sensuous things.

PG 4: 425.11 (25–6)
On: "to clear off from what differs more"[10]

They ascend from the sensuous to the intelligible, you understand.

PG 4: 425.11 (33–40)
On: "more 'life' and 'goodness' than 'air' and 'stone'"[11]

He properly exercises foresight over them. We have recounted them all in a different way in *On the Divine Names*. For since they are accidents, they are also all found in the substance of things beneath God. But God is over substance and is their cause. He is, then, over them as well. "Life" and "goodness," moreover, are affirmations or settings. "He does not get hungover, nor does he go mad" is a denial or clearing off.

PG 4: 428.3
On: "neither imagination, nor opinion, nor a word, nor intelligence"[12]

Imagination, opinion, reason, and intellection differ from one another as we contemplate them in the mind, as is shown above. Now we must consider that God does not possess reason like we possess reason. The same goes for the intellection found in intellective creatures, and we must expect the same of the other two. Our kind of knowing, moreover, must likewise be put with them. Dionysius says that we make settings of those — that is, creatures — that are beneath it — the divine nature, I mean — when we say "life" or "light" as we contemplate them in generated things. Using them, we consider the one who established them, but we do not introduce through them any setting down of his nature. In fact, we make a clearing off by saying that the divine is like none of them.

---

[9] See above, p. 89.
[10] See above, p. 91.
[11] See above, p. 91.
[12] See above, p. 101.

PG 4: 429.1 (9–11)
On: "nor deity"[13]

Gregory the Theologian, in the third of his *Theological Orations*, says that neither "divinity" nor "unbegotten" nor "fatherhood" signify the substance of God.

PG 4: 429.3 (1–6)
On: "it does not know realities"[14]

Do not let this chapter trouble you, so that you think that this man blasphemes the divine. His aim is to show that God is not a being, but is over beings. For if he produced all things by an act of creation, how could we discover that he was one particular being?

PG 4: 429.3 (21–8)
On the same passage

We grasp the intelligibles through learning, teaching, or illumination, but God does not know beings in any of these ways. He has an insight fitting for him. This is hinted at in the verse which runs: *who knew all things before they came to be.*[15] It shows that God knows beings not by the structure of their generation — that is, sensuously — but by another form of insight.

PG 4: 429.3 (32–41)
On the same passage

Moreover: beings — that is, creations — cannot extend themselves to intellections over their nature. Naturally, then, they do not know the divine nature as it is when they look into themselves. And so, then, the divine nature, when it looks into itself, does not know in itself the nature of beings in the structure of their substance. Dionysius shows this when he says "as realities are," for God exists over beings and over being itself in a manner over being. In no other way can we say that God does not know what he has created.

---

[13] See above, p. 103.
[14] See above, p. 107.
[15] Dan. 13: 42.

Appendix B: Related Scholia

PG 4: 33.10

On: "the simple summits of the heavenly hierarchies"[16]

This blessed man does not name at random, but properly, with much learning and piety. Since, then, he has said that our holy order is perfected through symbols that are material, discursive, and shaped into a figure fitting for us — and our ranking is an imitation of the order of holy angels — he has called our priesthood "summit." For those educated in these matters customarily call "summit" what is purest in each substance, and that on which the substance depends immediately — that is, intimately. For instance, the soul's ever so pure intellect is its summit, and the enflamed love of the higher and divine beings is the summit of love. What is most pure, then, and extended almost to immateriality in our hierarchy and mystery-laden order is the summit on which it depends. The summit of our figureless, simple, and bodiless mysteries is the most unsullied symbol, the human priesthood, on which stands the hierarchy joined to it. It ascends through images to the pure viewpoints of that intelligible rite we call the summit of the rites which here are bodily and of material form.

PG 4: 40.12

On: "unintelligible and indescribable limitlessness"[17]

He calls "unintelligible" not the crazy, but what no one intellects. Now God is limitless, since he does not submit to a limit. He is the limit of all things and he limits all things in himself, but he does not submit to a limit. Limits, then, accompany affirmations, but our affirmations of God are unfitting and false. God is over them, since he is not substance, but over substance.

PG 4: 41.1

On: "denials of divine things are true"[18]

He says that denials are true and affirmations unfitting not only for God but for everything divine — that is, for all the intelligibles beneath God. When we call God or the intellective powers "life" or "light," these affirmations are unfitting. For he is not some kind of life that lives through inhaling and exhaling, and he is not the light that

---

[16] *CH* 9, 14–5 (124A).
[17] *CH* 12, 20 (141A).
[18] *CH* 13, 1 (141A).

appears and makes objects visible. He is something higher than these. The denials we make through refusal are to some degree more akin to the intelligibles, for we say that they are "unseen" and that they do not submit to our vision. What the not apparent itself is, reason seems neither to care nor to establish. Indeed, "life" and "light" seem to signify what something is, but they do not at all show what God is.

PG 4: 216.1
On: "whatever belongs to the denial that overcomes"[19]

He glorifies what is over conception with a denial. For God is worshipped in the manner of an overcoming when we use what we cannot contemplate about him: such as the fact that he is immortal, that he is endless and invisible, and without need, and other things of this sort. For these, too, are common to the Trinity. Now causal names are whatever flowed into creation from God, who is the good cause of all things. As we find it written: *every good is his.*[20]

PG 4: 216.10
On: "all-knowable"[21]

We must say how God is both unknowable and all-knowable, and how we gain knowledge of him in unknowing. For God becomes known to unknowing. Now take "unknowing" not as the kind that arises through lack of learning, for that is a darkness of the soul, nor as the kind that understands that the unknowable is unknown, for this is a form of knowledge. Take it as the kind of unknowing by which the unknowable is known. By it we are simplified over all the intellections which, since they are multiplied and not one, scatter and gather us again. For this reason, then, we become simple when we overcome all intellection of God. We know nothing else, and we remain undifferentiated through our resting in unity, and we stalwartly rest in union. We do not know that we do not know — that is, we do not unknow like the unlearned, who know from something other than themselves, and so become able to learn what until then they did not know. We piously unknow what cannot be known by any reasoning creature. For when we rest in this unknowing, we become the form of the one who is before all things. When we abandon all forms and intellections, we are grounded in a speechlessness better than any utterance, by not knowing this: that we unknow. When we turn back again from this silence in speechlessness, and descend from muteness into utterance, and understand that we unknew, we draw back from seeking anything else about the unknowable. Now God is also called all-knowable because our thought of what he

---

[19] *DN* 125, 16 (640B).
[20] It is unclear what passage the scholiast means.
[21] *DN* 127, 1 (641A).

is arises from his lovingly given foresight and from his creations. From his foresight we think of him as savior. From his creations we think of him as creator. Dionysius calls the reality of God "setting down" since the being of all things arises from his reality. Now the philosophers also call "setting down" the forms set down in matter. Now they call "clearing off" when the qualities are cleared off the forms, like "heavy" from earth and "wet" from water. God, then, who causes even these transformations, is the setting down and clearing off of all things. He is the setting down of all things, since he sets down and makes them all and prepares their ground, for all things are established in him. Now he is the clearing off of all things, since he also transforms and refits the very setting down and making of beings. He clears off natural properties from what he has set down. For if we grant that what comes to be also completely decays — well he, by the wealth of his goodness, removes decay from some, like angels and souls, and changes decay into the undecaying and mortality into immortality in others, like our bodies in the resurrection. It is clear that the one who makes this real in us is himself over both setting down and clearing off. He is the foundation and root of all things, not spatially, but as their cause. He is not himself the clearing off of his possessions, since he possesses immortality itself. He has immortality, incomprehensibility, unknowability and things of this sort, not as though he were not their opposite. He has them by a kind of property that no one can describe or conceive, for he is removed from all things, since he is the clearing off of beings. Nothing in creation can think of or comprehend him, since he grasps himself through his own unlimitedness, for there is no limit to him. Now note that the divine subsistences are in each other by a kind of remaining and grounding. As we find it written: *I am in the Father and the Father is in me.*[22] The Apostle says the same thing about the Holy Spirit, too.

PG 4: 224.6
On: "if we should name 'God' the hiddenness over substance"[23]

That even the name "God" does not reveal his substance, nor what God is. It reveals a kind of good activity directed at us. Note also that we make names for God from participations given to us by God, but no one can conceive what God is. For the divine reality is worthily hymned to some degree when we free it altogether from all activity, both productive and intellective, and when it receives us in a holy silence, as we rush onto the gifts that radiate from it. For it produces beings by its will, standing us firmly in the undifferentiation of our mind, which he a little earlier called "knowing in unknowing."

---

[22] Ioh. 10:38.
[23] *DN* 131, 7–8 (645A).

PG 4: 244.7

On: "if the good is over all beings, and it is, then it gives form to the formless"[24]
See how privations in God — like "formless," "insubstantial," "lifeless" and "mindless"
— are overcomings productive of settings, for they contain the concept of not-being.
Nevertheless, they are thought to be in God by an overcoming, in a manner over being,
by the clearing off of all things, for God is not a being. Now Dionysius elucidates this
more perfectly in what follows.

PG 4: 245.3
On: "the divinity beyond all things"[25]

This is also in what he wrote above: that God both is in all things and is not any of
them. Now here he says more: that God is even over all substances. He says this below:
that God fills even not-beings. Now see how he says that those above do not come to
transcend it, and those below do not cross through it — that is, the divine has neither
beginning nor end. The heavenly and higher powers do not grasp it, because it is not,
and because it is not grasped. Do not think of it in this way, but think that it is not,
for this is "knowing in unknowing." For we who are higher, and are united through
divine love to the powers above — we know that, like everyone, we do not know the
divine nature.

PG 4: 264.1

On: "the intellective powers are useless when the soul, receiving the form of God"[26]
Note that mind is one thing and soul another. Dionysius calls intellections "intellective
activities and powers," which are lower, and a scattering of the mind. When the soul,
then, wishes to ascend to God and to be united to him so far as it can, it ought to turn
its eye — that is, the mind itself — away from particulars, and step up to more general things. Now intellections are particular, as I have said. Then, when the mind
becomes whole and turns to what is inside it, becoming oneness and simplicity, it will
be able to take to the divine rays through a praiseworthy unknowing, not the unknowing that arises from ignorance, but the unknowing that knows that it does not know
what cannot be grasped about God. As it enjoys the divine beams it will know not
through sensuous eyes — for God is not grasped by them — but by the eyeless estab-
lishments of the mind.

---

[24] *DN* 146, 6–7 (697A).
[25] *DN* 147, 4–5 (697C).
[26] *DN* 156, 17 (708D).

PG 4: 340.5

On: "it is customary to deny that privations are in God as oppositions"[27]

The aforesaid custom is for the theologians to apply privations to God so as to show opposition. We ought to think of it in this way: that they wished to establish, so far as they could, that the divine light which no one, whether immaterial or sensuous, can approach what is unapproachable and unseen, and so they named it darkness. As we find it written: *he made the shadows his refuge.*[28] The divine apostle puts it this way: *dwelling in unapproachable light.*[29] For what no one can approach is like the darkness which no one sees in its transcendence. Again, we find it written: *your understanding was marvelous to me. It was too strong. I am not able to reach it.*[30] And so, then, we glimpse the ungraspable and uncontrollably unintelligible understanding of God by an unknowing which transcends all the understanding in creatures. For the unknowing of what concerns God is not ignorance of the wise concerning divine things, but understanding, which knows in silence that God is unknowable. So, then, they call the incarnation of God the Word "emptying," even though he happens to be full, or rather overfull of wisdom, power, and salvation. They call the hanging on the cross the "weakness of God," since it is as though the wicked and unseen powers of the devil were dissolved by his death. And instead of death, a resurrection from the dead and the kingdom of heaven was established. The "foolishness of God," then, also functions in this way. God's thoughts transcend all human wisdom and understanding. Someone may understand what we have said in a heretical way, and I include the Hellenes among the heretics. They imagine that they can demonstrate with sensuous syllogisms that the incarnation of God, including his death, is impossible. To those who think this, the divine Paul, his head swimming, cries: *O the depth of the richness and wisdom of God! How inscrutable are his judgments!*[31] How, then, can foolish words untaught by God be equal to his method, which transcends all created wisdom? For the mystery cannot be explained in words or through sensuous demonstrations unless faith precedes.

PG 4: 341.1

On the same passage

As oppositions — that is, the contrary of the suffering Word. For the transcendence of God is shown through the denials that reveal the privations. He has elsewhere called this the power of transcendent denial.

---

[27] *DN* 193, 14–194, 1 (865B).
[28] Ps. 17:12.
[29] 1 Tim. 6:16.
[30] Ps. 139:6.
[31] Rom. 11:33.

PG 4: 352.2
On: "certain images and likenesses of his divine paradigms"[32]

Here the fore-definitions are taken as "divine paradigms," whose images are the products of creation. The Apostle called the fore-definitions "fore-settings," as he says in his letter to the Ephesians: *according to the fore-settings of the ages.*[33] God is known in every creature, you understand, as the artist in his works of art. What belongs to his substance, though, is altogether separate from all things. Although his works of art cannot know him in his substance, he is known by unknowing, just as he is known through the understanding grasp and insight of creatures. Taking up these matters again, then, he joins what follows together with the same topic.

PG 4: 352.3
On: "God is known through knowing and through unknowing"[34]

As he proceeds through them, he shows how God is understood through opposites, through settings, and through clearings. For he also said above, in the first chapter, that nothing can exhibit the substance of God: not intellection, not touch, not imagination, not opinion, nor the many things he has said here and there, which I also have interpreted while going through his works. Now he says that God is known through the renunciation of things here, though his substance is not known. To put it another way: nothing here can hold him so as to grasp him. Since, then, he is the cause of all things, he is known using what is from him. Now since he is not one of the things that are from him, he remains unknown to all. Now how he is also known through unknowing he also says here, and above, in the second chapter.

PG 4: 361.2
On: "he is not non-being"[35]

A denial set down against a denial makes an affirmation. When Dionysius says, then, that not-being is not in God, he gathers that God is. And so he says, then, that God is unable to be unable, just as he does not know how not to know. From this he gathers that God is altogether knowing and able. Now he does well to add "by privation" here. For "he is not able" and "he does not know" — these are not said in the manner of an overcoming, but a privation.

---

[32] *DN* 197, 21–2 (869D).
[33] Eph. 3:11.
[34] *DN* 198, 4 (872A).
[35] *DN* 203, 15 (893B).

Index of Names

Subject Index

Acephali, 19, 115

apophatic theology, *see* negative theology

clearing off (*ablatio*), 7, 27, 37–8, 63, 75, 77, 89, 91, 111, 116, 121

darkness

—is unapproachable light, 27, 123

—of God himself, 10, 18, 30, 33, 57, 65, 67, 69, 75

—of ignorance, 20, 120

—reduced to thought, 24

ecstasy, *see* surpassing

Expositions on the Heavenly Hierarchy, 2, 32

faculty of union, 11, 15

goodness, God as, 29, 85, 89, 91, 103, 105

infinite, God as, 31, 97, 109

mystery, 8, 27, 119, 123

negative theology, 28–30, 53, 81

Neoplatonists, 14, 20

Nestorians, 19, 115

On the Divine Names, 3, 4, 5–6, 7, 8, 11, 12, 13, 20, 21, 29, 34, 35, 59, 63, 69, 77, 87, 116

On Divine Predestination, 1

On the Ecclesiastical Hierarchy, 8, 23, 34

On the Heavenly Hierarchy, 3, 8, 23, 33, 34, 63, 69

onrush (*epibole*), 11, 12–5, 20, 24

over-being, 8, 10, 28–9, 51, 53, 75

over-god, 28–9, 37, 51, 53

Passion of St. Dionysius, 5, 32, 36

Periphyseon, 2, 3, 22, 23, 28, 30, 31, 32, 34, 35, 36

place

—Aristotelian category of, 14, 31, 109

—of God, 10–1, 24, 67, 69

—symbolic name, 6, 87, 97

purification, 9, 67, 103

quantity, Aristotelian category of, 31, 95, 109

Renaissance, 3, 15, 32

scholia, Dionysian

—authorship, 16

—Neoplatonic influences, 19–20

—translation into Latin, 2, 26–7

—transmission history, 16–8

sense, interior, 101

senses, spiritual, 15

setting down (*positio*), 27, 37–8, 63, 77, 89, 91, 111, 116, 120–1, 124

silence, 9, 25, 57, 109, 120, 123

summit, 10, 23–4, 25, 65, 67, 69, 111

surpassing (*excessus*), 22, 59

Symbolic Theology, 4, 6–7, 81, 87, 115

Theological Characters, 4, 5, 7, 9, 85, 87